and
Milestones

# A Teenager's Diary of Moving on from **Anorexia**

## Mealtimes and Milestones

Constance Barter

**ROBINSON**
London

Constable & Robinson Ltd
3 The Lanchesters
162 Fulham Palace Road
London W6 9ER
www.constablerobinson.com

First published in the UK by Robinson,
an imprint of Constable & Robinson Ltd, 2010

A copy of the British Library Cataloguing in
Publication data is available from the British Library

ISBN: 978-1-84901-323-9

Printed and bound in the EU

1 3 5 7 9 10 8 6 4 2

# IN MEMORY OF CLIVE BARTER

*Dad, you saw me through recovery, but never saw this book.*
*You're the angel looking over me.*
*xxx*

Hope is always
THERE... except when
you don't believe it.
PAUSE
That's when other people step
in and hold it for you.

*A picture that I did in my last Creative Group on my final day*

# ACKNOWLEDGEMENTS

My thanks go to my fabulous mum, who never lost her temper, but more importantly never lost her hope.

To Broo, Fritha and Phillipa and all the other amazing people involved, who believed in *Mealtimes and Milestones* and made it happen.

To my family – Granny and Granddad, Simon and Mandy. Small family. Big love.

To the professionals around me – from my tutor to my out-patient team, and all the others in between.

Finally to my friends, who definitely kept the postman busy with all their letters, cards, drawings, photographs, quotes from *Friends*, prayers, handmade bracelets, surfing books and Sudoku puzzles! It was your plentiful words of inspiration that made me smile and helped pull me through. xxx

# FOREWORD

I was very pleased and honoured to be asked to provide this foreword. It is always a pleasure to see someone beat their eating disorder, and that pleasure is all the greater when they are able to help others do the same by sharing their experiences.

With this book, Constance has given a remarkable account of her journey to recovery. We know it takes courage, determination and great persistence – qualities that Constance has in abundance. That she has been able to share her insights in such a forthright and honest way is particularly powerful.

Beat (the Eating Disorders Association) is the UK's leading charity supporting people affected by eating disorders and campaigning on their behalf. We provide individuals and their families with support, information and encouragement to seek recovery. We collaborate with leading researchers, and provide professional development for health, education and social care staff. Our web presence is extensive, and broadcasters and journalists turn to us daily for comment and opinion.

Our message is simple: eating disorders will be beaten. They will be beaten when they are no longer misunderstood, trivialized or seen as something to be ashamed of.

Eating disorders are a serious type of mental illness that takes a tremendous toll on promising young lives. They can be deadly: 20 per cent of those who become seriously affected die as a result. Eating disorders can affect anyone at any age, including boys and men, but girls and young women aged between 12 and 20 are most at risk.

Anorexia nervosa is the rarest of the eating disorders, accounting for only 10 per cent of cases; but it is also the most serious in terms of its potential long-term consequences for physical health and well-being if not treated quickly and effectively.

We are learning more all the time about what causes eating disorders. The causes are complex, and it is a combination of factors that makes some people vulnerable. There is world-class research in this field, much of it conducted in the UK, helping to build an evidence base for understanding this condition and helping effective treatments to be developed. One of the things this research is showing is that more of the risks are 'hard-wired' than was previously thought. Our genetic make-up, personality type, brain chemistry and hormones all play a part.

Beat campaigns to change the way everyone thinks and talks about eating disorders, helping to overcome the stigma caused by mistaken views and outdated opinions. Explaining the scientific knowledge we have gained is part of that.

We challenge the media to tell the truth about eating disorders. They are not a fad or a phase or a silly diet gone wrong. They are not about trying to emulate celebrities or fashion. We want everyone with an eating disorder to truly believe they can beat it. We know that the sooner someone gets the specialist treatment they need the more likely they are to make a full recovery. We also know that people can be very reluctant to ask for or accept that help – even once they know they need it – such are the feelings of worthlessness an eating disorder produces.

We want a message of hope – that eating disorders *can* be beaten – to reach anyone and everyone who needs to hear it. Constance's story is a hugely powerful expression of that message – that hope.

*Susan Ringwood*
Chief Executive
Beat

# INTRODUCTION

It is both an honour and a privilege to have been asked to provide this introduction to *Mealtimes and Milestones*. Anorexia nervosa remains an illness that is hard to understand, for sufferers, families and professionals alike, and misunderstandings about it abound. This is not surprising, for it is, by its nature, an illness that causes confusion, mystification, distortion and puzzlement. It is not surprising, therefore, that its portrayal in the media often focuses on superficial and ultimately misleading issues, which in turn often contributes to those suffering from it feeling misunderstood. As those closest to it know, it is not just about food and weight, but strikes at the very heart of a person's selfhood and their relationship with the world around them, and often leaves them feeling hopeless and alone.

Although there has been a considerable increase in knowledge about anorexia nervosa over the past two decades, there is still much to learn. It does not matter how many clever and highly sophisticated scientific research studies are done, there is still no substitute for learning from those who know most about the experience of having it: that is, those who suffer from it. This most particularly applies to the provision of treatment. Unless we are aware of the experience of people going through treatment and how it affects them, we are unlikely to develop treatments that will be effective in the long run. *Mealtimes and Milestones* gives an astonishingly courageous and frank account of one person's journey towards recovery. In doing this, the author provides profound insights into the way anorexia makes young people think and into the way it can distort their perception of the world.

One of the most difficult things about suffering from anorexia nervosa, and about having a member of your family suffer from it, is the way it undermines and threatens to destroy hope. The anorexic inner 'voice' is so determined not to relinquish control, so determined to maintain its grip, that any sign of hopefulness, or move towards recovery, is mercilessly attacked from within. For me, the most important feature of this book is the way Constance describes how she moved from a position of near-hopelessness to a position in which hope was regained and then allowed to flourish. For those who are currently stuck in a position of hope-lessness, this book is likely to bring great comfort, not only to them but also to their families. It shows that whatever you think at the time, anorexia *can* be left behind; that no matter how dark the night, the dawn will come, provided there is someone involved who is able to hold on to hope.

As I suspect all professionals know, those suffering from an illness like anorexia are much more likely to listen to those who have been through it themselves than they are to listen to professionals. This is not surprising, indeed it is to be expected; after all, most of us find it easier to accept advice from someone if we feel they have personal experience of any particular situation. It is therefore likely that reading this book will play a significant part in helping someone suffering from anorexia nervosa to take their courage in both hands, as Constance has done, and allow themselves the hope that they can and will recover if they are willing to work at it.

I am extremely grateful to Constance for having the courage and generosity to share her experience with others. I suspect it could not have been an easy decision for her, particularly as her journey is inevitably a very personal one. The fact that she has done so is a testament to how far she has come on her own journey. My hope is that those who read of her struggles, and who are in the midst of those struggles themselves (either as a sufferer or as relative, friend or supporter of a sufferer), will be able to identify with her, and with her courage and tenacity, and that doing so will play a significant part in enabling them to find their own way out of the darkness.

*David Wood FRCPsych*
Consultant Child and Adolescent Psychiatrist
Clinical Director, The Ellern Mede Centre for Eating Disorders

# THE BEGINNING
## July 2007

'Constance, you've lost loads of weight.'

People are noticing me. My friends have never really seen me before. Now finally I am being recognized by them – and they like me because I am thin.

This was perhaps the first time I made the connection between thinness and happiness – and I loved this new-found power. Starving myself gave me a power and a real feeling of excitement that I had never experienced before.

Maybe my eating disorder was a predisposition within me, maybe it was a manifestation of my inner insecurities, or maybe there weren't any specific triggers. I am now 16 years old, and my anorexia was diagnosed when I was 14, yet I can remember from as young as 11 or 12 years old wanting to be physically fit. I would carry my school bag, sports bag and violin up to school all at once, instead of going on the bus, in an attempt to make myself stronger. At that stage I hadn't made the connection between exercise and weight loss, and an unhealthy relationship with food didn't arrive until I was 13, but the foundations were certainly there.

3

Thinking back, I can't pinpoint exactly every part of my life which could possibly have contributed to my eating disorder – and it would be unrealistic to try. But I have always worked to the best of my ability, and even at a young age I would stay up late to make sure that a piece of homework was perfect. Before anorexia overtook my life, it must have been perfectionism and an inbuilt highly driven trait within me that led me to these extremes, because no one taught me or told me to do this.

I have had a very happy and stable upbringing, and have always been loved and had positive reinforcement, yet I still had many gnawing insecurities about my likeability and talents. I never felt I was good enough, even when I got an A grade. I guess sooner or later these doubts had to reveal themselves, because no one can possibly hide them for ever.

I was bullied at my junior school, but my current school was the one I have always wanted to go to, and I absolutely loved it. I started off as a day pupil, but enjoyed school life so much that I started boarding one night a week, then two. By the end of the first term I was a weekly boarder.

It was at school that I developed an interest in running, and I ran for the county, but I quickly realized that I could use it to lose weight. Perfect. People would just think that I was training. I set a mental programme for myself. Each week the distance would increase – and the percentage for my enjoyment became lower and lower. It wasn't for me any more; instead it was for the voice getting louder and louder inside my head, punishing me if I didn't comply. Eventually I was running around 25 km a week and swimming around 6 km – on only half a yoghurt and a cherry tomato a day. But how did it get to that stage?

The voice crawled in gradually, but quickly tightened its grip.

*'It's easy,'* it told me. *'Just do it really slowly and no one will notice.'* A whole jacket potato soon became half, then a quarter. Salad became a leaf or two. I would follow this restricting pattern in the week, but then I would eat 'normally' at the weekend, so that my parents wouldn't notice. It was the perfect plan.

Finally my lack of eating and excessive exercise became apparent to people around me. They would say that it wasn't normal to do this amount of exercise.

'Yes it is.'

'Are you anorexic?'

'No, you liar.'

I didn't want to believe them. They were lying, they were meant to be my friends, but they were just trying to make me fat. I hate them. I HATE THEM.

But they knew something was wrong, and were very concerned about how much I was exercising. Eventually they took my running shorts and hid them from me to try to stop me from going out running.

By that time I'd started to faint at school. The first time it happened I had just come back from a run. I was in my room on my own, and my sight became blurred, and black circles took over my vision. The black circles in front of my eyes were like the anorexia on my mind, distorting the truth. Of course I was scared, but I was even more scared to tell anyone.

*'If you say anything I will punish you, you'll regret it, keep yourself to yourself, they don't understand. They don't like you either.'*

I fainted again later on in the week, and I was light-headed. I begged my friends not to say anything to the teachers, but they did.

*'See . . . they've betrayed you . . . I would never do that to you. I saw you and befriended you when they didn't want you.'*

This was true. The voice had picked me up when I was low, and convinced me that I was invincible; why should I think that it was lying to me?

Later on, the school matron came to see me. At first I was really closed off to her.

*'Don't tell her anything.'*

Despite what the voice was telling me I did admit about the collapsing. She told me to wait in my room and not to leave. I felt angry and alone. And now my one friend was punishing me too.

*'Look what you did . . . you stupid, idiot girl. You are nothing. I hate you too now.'*

'No, please don't leave me, I'm sorry, you're all I've got,' I cried to myself in my room. In a short amount of time I had become reliant on this imaginary, deceiving person, and I couldn't get out of this loop. It was my one friend.

I felt that no one could understand me, and I didn't want to talk to anyone because I was afraid that they would laugh at me. No one could understand what was going on in my head. I had admitted about the fainting, but I was never going to confess about the voice.

Matron and my house parents told me to go and see the school doctor. He made me feel really uncomfortable and put me completely out of my comfort zone. He weighed me and measured my height. My BMI[1] was obviously low and he said that by the end of the next school holidays he wanted me to have put weight

---

[1] BMI stands for Body Mass Index – a measurement used by doctors to calculate whether someone's weight is healthy for their height.

on. He also banned me from doing sport. However, this just accelerated the anorexia, because if I couldn't lose weight by exercising I had to restrict my food intake even more.

*'See . . . they are all betraying you . . . I am your true friend.'*

I began to hate everyone around me. I felt on my own. In desperation I started to make myself sick. I couldn't see any other way. The packed lunch would be given to me, and I would open up the packets of chocolate, crisps and sandwiches, to make it look like I had eaten something – and then throw it all in the bin. When dinner came, I ate about half of it – I was so hungry, I hadn't eaten properly in so long, but then in comes . . .

*'What have you done? You've got to get rid of it.'*

I had to do it, I had no choice. I went into the toilet and just made myself sick. It was an awful experience. I sank to the floor after I did it and sobbed alone in the dark. I knew this wasn't normal, but I had to get rid of the toxic food that I had just eaten. There was no other option. The voice even congratulated me afterwards for doing it.

In a matter of only a few months it had taken over my life. I would do anything for anorexia to please it. It destroyed any hope and inner strength that I had, and it stopped me from accepting help and seeing who I really was, and how physically and mentally ill I was. I continually doubted myself, and many times through this journey I doubted the point of my life. I was never good enough and I always put myself down. I felt like I was screaming out my pain and loneliness, but the sound of my misery was buried and trapped deep within me.

It picked me up because I couldn't control this feeling of failure which always followed me, and so the only way I could gain self-confidence was to starve myself. But I sank further and further into myself. I isolated myself from others and was in complete denial that anything was wrong.

My body was so weak. Every single muscle ached. It got to the stage where all I could do was lie on a sofa and rest. Whenever I tried to stand up I would just collapse. But all I could think about was how this was making me a better person.

Eventually Mum took me to our local hospital. By this point I was refusing not only to eat but, more worryingly, to drink anything at all.

*'Keep going . . . you're doing so well.'*

I was cross with her for taking me, but also relieved because my anorexia told me I was being recognized as a 'good anorexic'. Finally I had something to identify myself by. I continued to refuse all nourishment, despite endless support from my parents and the hospital staff, until the point came when they had to act: I was delirious and my heart was beginning to slow down.

Refusing water was my ultimate weapon. They even gave me a little medicine measuring cup, and tried to make me drink a sip an hour. But I couldn't do it. I just couldn't.

*'It will make you fat . . . don't do it . . . they're trying to trick you.'*

I stayed there for a week with a drip in my arm. Then I was transferred to a specialized eating disorders unit for adolescents.

I remember being so scared while driving to the unit, but I didn't cry. I didn't have the strength to cry.

At the unit I joined around fifteen other young people from all over the country, all of whom were also in-patients. I tried to think about it as like the first day of a new school term. The difference was that this time I didn't know how long the term would be. Would I be there for weeks, months or years?

Going into hospital as an in-patient, although it was such a gruelling experience, helped me to break this defensive anorexic shell and re-emerge as a more confident person – to realize that I am who I am, and I don't have to compare myself with anyone.

I was admitted on Tuesday 17 July 2007 and I was there for seven months. This is the diary that I wrote, starting in August.

# THE DIARY
**Thursday 9 August 2007 to**
**Thursday 14 February 2008**

## Thursday 9 August

Weighing today. I really hate it. I just get so anxious. Have I put on weight? Have I lost weight?

In the past I have usually had about two good weeks followed by three or four bad days. This pattern has almost become a habit, but where have the bad days gone? Shouldn't they have come by now? I suppose I might be getting better! But how come? I'm not ready to get better. I still need to get thin. I can't accept this, I can't. The voice told me, and planned that I wasn't going to eat. It told me that if I put on weight, that could be my excuse to starve myself again. It told me not to worry if I had put on weight this time, because I will soon be able to lose it again. It told me – so I have to believe it.

I went down, undressed, got on the scales and waited for the three numbers to come up. Yes, I had only put on a tiny amount, but it felt enough to blame myself for.

Breakfast was put in front of me.

*'No, don't give in, you mustn't. Do NOT put it in your mouth.'*

I kept telling myself this over and over again. Then I figured there was no point in not eating but still drinking, it didn't have enough impact for me, I had to not drink either. I was so tempted the whole time, but I just kept saying to myself that it was for the best.

For the morning activity someone came in to teach us drama. But to be honest I wasn't really concentrating, I was preoccupied with thinking about food and water.

Snacks.[1] Resisting my snacks felt so good, because they looked really nice. I pulled them closer to myself to make it look like I was trying, but I wasn't going to have any.

At lunch I got to the stage of cutting the smallest piece of broccoli off. I got it halfway to my mouth, but then stopped . . .

*'DON'T GIVE IN!'* it shouted at me.

I had a core team[2] meeting today. My key worker[3] brought up my eating today, and asked what was going on. God, I really wish she hadn't. I just want to forget about it and get out of here. When they asked me how they could help me, I just didn't know. I have

---

[1] There was a set sequence of eating times in the unit: breakfast, morning snacks, lunch, afternoon snacks, tea, and late snacks. These were usually taken in the dining room, at tables of about six young people with a member of staff at either end.

[2] Your core team is the group of staff directly associated with your treatment plan (key workers, therapist, case manager and key teacher).

[3] The key worker is one of two members of staff who work directly with you and your treatment plan.

wound myself up so deeply. I have dug such a big hole and there doesn't seem to be a ladder around to get myself out, and I don't really want to find that ladder. I'd planned to gain some self-confidence today through not eating, but now anorexia had taken over, and I wasn't in control any more. It isn't up to me, I just have to obey my illness.

I only managed a few sips of water at afternoon snacks. I was feeling so trapped. Anorexia had taken control, and I didn't know how to get out. I was so hungry, but it just kept telling me:

*'This is a good thing. Keep going. Never give in. Hunger is your friend; it means that you are losing weight.'*

It took a lot of encouragement from staff just to make me take those few sips. Afterwards I felt terrible. Everything had just become out of proportion.

Afterwards, I had a meeting with two senior members of staff. They explained very bluntly that they would have to pass a tube[4] if I carried on not eating or drinking. This put me in such a big mess, I was so confused about what to do, I had so many thoughts and feelings:

*'You want the tube because it gets the message across, it means you are ill.'*

'What? . . . No you don't, it's painful and unnecessary, you don't need to go down that road.'

'Just eat, Constance, you can do this, you are hungry and thirsty.'

---

[4] The 'tube' or 'NG tube' is a naso-gastric tube that is passed through the nose down into the stomach and is used to help feed someone who isn't eating or drinking enough by mouth.

All these thoughts were running through my head and I just didn't know which one to choose. I had already taken the decision to let anorexia take control, and that clearly was the wrong decision, but then again, it was making me thin so that is the best thing that has ever happened to me.

In my core team they decided to let me have a phone call with a friend, but I couldn't get through, so I had to leave a message. I just said that it would be great to talk to her and catch up if she wanted to give me a call back. I was quite nervous, because part of me was really ashamed of being in hospital and I didn't want my friends to feel burdened with my feelings.

I only managed six sips of water at tea. By now I was feeling really weak when I stood up and I really wanted to give in, but I knew that I couldn't. I felt guilty too, because the staff were giving me so much support, and were really encouraging me, and I could see how it was affecting the rest of the young people.

My friend rang me back after tea. It was really good to speak to her and just to hear a friend's voice. For thirteen minutes I felt healthy, and that I could recover. It gave me real motivation – but just as quickly as the motivation came, it went when she hung up the phone.

I had a session with my key worker this evening, and I shared some things which were really close to me. I just don't see the point of living any more. I feel worthless. I'm not any good at anything. I find it so hard to want to put anything inside me like food and water because I am no good. I don't deserve it. I'm nothing, so it is easier and better to have nothing inside me. My key worker asked me to think of three good things about me, but I can't think of any.

I had the same conversation with my mum in my phone call.[5] She said that she had quite broad shoulders, but I think that it was hard for her to hear that her daughter just wants to die. So much of this illness is behind closed doors. I bet most people can't imagine what it is like to feel this way. Imagine if my friends at school knew the real truth – that their friend is in a state of mind where she can't see a way out. The voice keeps telling me that death is the only option. I have reached rock bottom, and I can't see any hope. I am super-glued into a hole.

I was obviously quite distressed about my phone call, so it didn't help that I had to go straight into evening snacks afterwards. I walked into the dining room and just burst into tears. I didn't know how to cope. When I'm upset or confused my first combat reaction is just to starve myself.

I'm going to bed early so I can just get to sleep and forget the day, and drift away. If only it could be a reality.

## Friday 10 August

I woke up this morning in a new frame of mind. I was going to do this, beat anorexia and not have a tube. This unfortunately went as soon as breakfast was put in front of me. My confidence and strong will were shattered once again by anorexia. It had blown things totally out of proportion. I had a few sips but this seemed like a gallon of water. I guess this is how it takes control and is so deadly because it makes you believe that you are having more than you actually are.

During team games my key worker called me inside. I knew from the minute she called my name that it was either about having

---

[5] I had two thirty-minute phone calls home each week.

a naso-gastric tube inserted now, or discussing when it would be put in. She had spoken to my parents, and they had given permission for a tube to be passed. I am so cross because I don't want to live any more, I just want to starve myself to death, I don't see why I am still here. It would be better if I wasn't here because I am such a burden on everyone.

*'You're nothing, a total waste of space.'*

What is the point of my life any more?

She had also spoken to the nurses and they had taken the decision to pass a tube at 10.45 a.m., unless I could eat all of my morning snacks.

I burst into tears again at snacks. My key worker walked down the hall with me into the dining room and sat down next to me. Even more thoughts were running through my head – not running, these were sprinting. I wanted the tube, I didn't want the tube, eat – I was starving – don't you just want to die, don't give in and end your life, you are never going to recover, but they won't let you do that. HELP!! . . .

When 10.45 a.m. came, I had managed a bite of my snacks. The nurse then walked in, and because I had made a start the decision was made to let me have until 11 a.m., but then they would tube me. I just cried and cried. I felt like all the emotions that I had felt over the last few days were just coming up in buckets and buckets of tears. I was totally helpless, I couldn't help myself, and I couldn't accept help – anorexia wouldn't let me. They gave me the last option which was to drink my snack in Enlive,[6] but I just couldn't . . .

---

[6] Enlive is a nutritious feeding liquid.

18

They basically had to drag me out of the dining room. I had to sit down on the treatment room bed. This was it. I was having the thing I least wanted, but also what my anorexia most wished for.

One member of staff took the tube and measured it against my body to see roughly where my stomach was. While my key worker held my hand, she told me that she would push it up my nose, and then it would go down the back of my throat and then into my stomach. She moved the tube nearer and nearer my nose. I moved away, so she had to support my head. I was crying and groaning, but through my tears I begged her not to do it. 'Let me die, I'm worthless.' This wasn't my anorexia saying this, though . . . this was me now.

I thought about what my friends would be doing at that moment. Having fun at school, laughing with friends, enjoying life – and here I was, having a tube inserted into my stomach.

To make it smoother going down they suggest that you take a gulp of water, so when it goes down the water opens up the passages. I didn't want to have it, but I had it anyway just to try and make it more comfortable. She pushed the tube up my nose and then said the word 'gulp'. I swallowed the water and the stiff tube went down with it. It was awful. For one thing, I didn't want to live, and two, it was like I could actually feel the tube going down inside me and moving. She then taped the rest to the side of my face and round the back of my ear.

It was then time for my first feed via an NG tube. They syringed up the Enlive, attached it to my tube and then pushed it down. I could actually feel my stomach filling up but nothing was entering my mouth. I felt really light-headed and I vomited. They got me to do breathing exercises to try to calm me down. It helped a bit

19

but I still hated the sensation, and I wondered how long I would have to go through this for.

I ate some lunch, but it was really uncomfortable with the tube in my throat. It feels like when you don't chew a large piece of food enough, and you can feel it go down your throat. You keep swallowing and eventually it moves down and you can't feel it any more, but the tube doesn't move, and it stays there.

In Friday Group[7] one of the things talked about was the low mood, which was partly because of people not eating. I feel like all the young people are really mad with me, and that I have caused the entire low mood. One of the young people actually directed a question at me.

'I wonder how it feels for Constance hearing this?'

There was a long silence where I wondered whether to respond.

'Yeah, it is quite hard, because when people talk about the non-eating, that is basically me, so I just feel like I take all of the responsibility, and I'm so sorry that I have affected you all so much.'

There was another long silence, then another young person responded.

'It's just hard when other people don't eat, because none of us want to, but sometimes you just have to.'

The conversation then moved on. I just feel so guilty though. I don't want to affect other people, but I also don't want to eat.

For the rest of the day I just had to keep thinking that the more I ate normally the less I had to have through my tube. It was such

---

[7] Friday Group takes place every Friday and involves the whole community. The young people get an opportunity to talk among themselves, with the staff listening but not saying anything. Then it swaps round, and the young people listen to the staff. Finally everyone comes together and talks.

a struggle, with every snack and every meal. One of the staff members was lovely and offered loads of support as she could see that I was finding it really hard. She asked me why, but I just kept crying and saying that I didn't see why people were being so supportive, when all I wanted to do was end my life. She kept reiterating that I DID deserve to live, and I DID deserve food, and I DID mean something to many people. I tried to believe this but I just couldn't, it was too hard, and a complete lie to me. It's all a lie.

## Saturday 11 August

My parents arrived at 10 a.m. for their visit today.[8] I had to get my tube re-stuck on as the tape wasn't sticky any more, so they were waiting in reception for me. When I opened the door I found it really awkward. I knew that they were slightly anxious about seeing me in case I was angry with them for giving permission to pass the NG tube. To be honest, I am a bit, but I was just so glad to see them. Whenever something painful has happened to me before Mum has always been there holding my hand, but this time she hadn't been there, which makes me feel even more lonely.

When I left them to go into morning snacks, instead of having a green snack, I changed it for a blue and a red;[9] this was more manageable for me, because it enabled me to have smaller mouthfuls. For me, it is more about the portion size, and not the calories, but while I have been here I seem to have developed an obsession with calories, because here everything is so calorie

---

[8] My parents visited me on Saturdays, for most of the day. At first they spent the time with me in the unit; later on I was able to go out with them for the afternoon.

[9] Different colours are used to correspond to different calorific amounts. A green snack is the same as a red and a blue snack together.

controlled – it's hard to avoid getting caught up in it. I guess I didn't count them before because there wasn't any real option at school to know the calorific amount in the food; I just went on portion size, as that was much easier to reduce.

I've tried different methods to disguise food for myself while I've been in the unit, to try to make myself think I'm eating less than I am, so I won't get distressed about it. One thing I do is wrap food up in other types of food. I did this at snacks this morning. I put pieces of chocolate inside a dried apricot. I guess I was trying to trick my mind into thinking I was having less than I actually was. I finished my snack, but my guilty feelings just became too great. I walked out of the dining room and shut myself in the toilet. I couldn't believe I had been so stupid as to give in.

*'You're a failure. You've betrayed me.'*

I didn't deserve to eat food. So much for wanting to end my life; I had just got as far as possible away from doing that.

*'You stupid, stupid girl, you deserve to die, you're nothing, nothing.'*

The voice kept on and on at me.

I tried to compose myself as I went back to join my parents, but one of the nurses had seen that I had been crying and called me back and asked if I wanted to talk. We sat down, and I just felt all of the emotions come back up again. I didn't know what to do but cry. I possess so much self-hatred. I just want all these pressuring thoughts to disappear, and I want to be able to eat some food, even a snack, without feeling the need to commit suicide afterwards. Is that really so much to ask for? My parents had seen me talking to the nurse so when I went back Mum opened her arms out to me and gave me a big hug. I burst into tears again. I am fed up of this illness, I just

22

want it to leave me alone, I want Mum to click her fingers and it all to go away, but it is never going to be that simple, and the road of recovery that lies ahead of me is very long, very hard and very frightening if I choose to take it, and I am scared of embarking on it.

Mum and Dad left at 5.45 p.m. I was incredibly sad that they were leaving but also glad because they are quite 'lovey-dovey' parents, and because I am so self-conscious about my body I don't really feel comfortable with hugs, so I always get cross, but I don't feel strong enough to say that to them in case they become cross with me. I would rather have a swift exit than a ten-minute goodbye. I want to exert independence, and I don't appreciate that much affection, especially when I want to die anyway. I know I should be able to accept affection, but I just find it too hard.

I ate about a third of my tea, but then I had to wait for my feed by tube, which just increased my anxieties. It was so much today, I was really down on calories. I cried the whole time that the nurse was feeding me. I know that this isn't what I want in my life. I just want to escape and never return.

I got a text from one of my friends tonight and it said:

---

TEXT MESSAGE:
Babe. There is always a tunnel out. ALWAYS. You have just got to wait until you find it – Which will be very soon. Everything will seem better soon. Keep the faith babe. xxx

---

I just found that so inspirational, and I was really proud to be friends with someone so supportive, and things like that give me glimmers of hope, which I really need right now.

## Sunday 12 August

I really wanted to go to church this morning. I just find it really helpful. It gives me an hour of peace. I find prayer very beneficial, and I believe that if you believe enough, God will answer your prayers. I used to go to church a lot with my dad when I was younger, but then I stopped. But since I've been ill, I've been praying a lot more, before I go to sleep.

You have to be up to date,[10] though, to go to church, and that is what got me through breakfast. I just had to give myself a chance to show myself that I did deserve to live. At the end of breakfast I still didn't think that I deserved my life, but at least I had managed a meal.

One of the nurses came over and said that they were pleased that I had completed breakfast, and that church had motivated me, but they were concerned about how the rest of the day would turn out, because to be up to date before church I actually only needed to eat breakfast because we would leave at 10 a.m.

She also wanted to talk to me about tomorrow's trip to Willen Lake, one of the activity trips that take place in the summer holidays. You can do canoeing, low ropes, high ropes,[11] orienteering, etc. I would be restricted anyway on some of the activities because of my tube. She also reminded me that the tube would only come out once I'd been completely up to date for three whole days – they didn't want to take it out and then have to put it back in because it's quite an intrusive procedure.

---

[10] Being 'up to date' means having kept up with your daily meal plan.

[11] 'Low ropes' is an obstacle course near the ground; 'high ropes' is the same kind of course, but higher off the ground.

She said that she would allow me to go to church though.

I did have mixed feelings about going to church with my tube because I was afraid people would stare at me. On one side I am very ashamed of having a tube because it shows that I have given up the fight, but I'm also proud of it because it shows me that I am doing well at being the 'best anorexic'. Although it was embarrassing I did wonder what people were thinking when they saw me . . . and yes, people did stare.

When we got back for snacks, I felt an enormous amount of pressure because I wanted to try to prove to the staff that I did deserve to go to church. It was very hard as usual, but I did manage it.

When I got to lunch, though, I just broke down. I couldn't keep going. I had eaten breakfast and snacks and I just couldn't face lunch. At first I even found it hard to look at the plate, but slowly I managed to see that eating it orally would be much less painful than being fed through the tube, and eventually made a start. I was shocked and annoyed, though, that I didn't receive any support from the nurse. I don't know if it was on purpose, but I just found it strange, because she could see that I was crying and obviously distressed. When I asked for a tissue the student nurse brought them over. She put the box next to me and I took one, but then the nurse said, 'No, take the box away.' I got the impression that either she was seeing what I could do on my own or she was cross with me because she had allowed me to go to church and now I was struggling to eat lunch.

I ate most of it, but I couldn't get on to my pudding, even though I knew that meant I'd have to have a feed by tube and I didn't want it to happen.

I tried the wrapping method again at snacks, but I was concerned because I couldn't see the actual amount of calories on the packet. It has become an obsession. If I don't know I become more scared. What if I put something high in calories in my body which I don't deserve?

I talked with one of the nurses between snacks and tea. I said that I found going to church really helpful because it got me through breakfast, but afterwards I felt a huge burden of pressure to go on eating to prove that I'd deserved to go, but also pressure from my anorexia *not* to eat. I really want to get better, I know I do, but I can't. I just can't. There's no hope for me. It is pointless trying because it is just going to be another thing on the long list of things that I am going to fail at. It doesn't make sense when people say differently.

I was worried about tea because I just kept reflecting on what I had eaten, and it seemed so daunting that yet again I was going to have to force more food inside me. It's fuel, but also my poison. The nurse reassured me that I can only do my best, but I didn't want to let that train of thought make me not eat anything, because I know that it's just going to be fed to me through a tube anyway.

It was sandwiches for tea. It was as hard as I expected. I kept adding up all the food in my stomach, all that repulsive, toxic, sickly stuff that you have to put inside you. I didn't want my pudding given to me. I couldn't even look at the food because it terrified me so much. I could see what I had to do. It's a natural process, but it was all too much. Just the one sandwich seemed like a mountain on a plate. I have this very strong image in my head which has been with me for a very long time and therefore is deeply planted in my head. It's of a flat abdomen – it's already

Dear Connie

I Just want you to NO how amazing I think you are one of the most gantastic People I have met you are an insperation to me and everyone.
I want you to know that if you ever need anything I am alway here I will always be there to look out for you.
I No that things are going to be hard But I know is there is any one who can get through this it is you.
Whatever you do you never seem to sail that is how I know you can do it
your one of my closest griends and I know I can talk to you about any thing and I thank you for That.

*A letter from one of my school friends*

full of your guts and stomach, so eating just expands it, and that's exactly why I don't want to eat.

Before evening snacks I got talking to one of the other young people which I really enjoyed and we were able to share our experiences. She finds it hard to go into the dining room, so I offered to hold her hand, and I sat with her and offered her support. I enjoyed the evening because we could relate to each other and exchange support. It upsets me that such a lovely girl is struggling with this illness. It's a stupid, destroying illness which no one should have to go through, but this is what I deserve, so I just have to live with that.

## Monday 13 August

It was weighing today. It's always so hard, but today I was quietly confident that I had lost weight. Even though the hospital didn't want that, I want to feel like my efforts of starvation have paid off. And they had, so I finally felt proud of myself, something that I haven't felt in a long time. I know in the back of my mind that I can't be proud of this, but I am, and I can't help this.

The first activity at Willen Lake was 'Katakanu'. It's a six-person canoe. It was really good fun, but it brought back feelings about exercise, and how I'm not allowed to do much now. I found it really frustrating, because it made me just want to go running and let all my troubles fall away, but I managed to put these thoughts out of my mind and I was just thankful to be out of the hospital for a day.

We sat down on the grass to have lunch. I hadn't been to Willen Lake before, and this was my first meal out in public. One nurse positioned herself so people couldn't see my tube, which was helpful. I couldn't manage it all, I couldn't find the motivation. Technically, because I didn't eat everything and wasn't up to date, I wasn't allowed to go on the low ropes, but the decision was made to let me go anyway. Although I was grateful, it made me wonder – does it mean I can get away with other things as well?

The low ropes course reminded me a bit of my struggle with anorexia. The whole course was hard, but some bits were so hard that I needed help and support from other people to be able to cross the bridge and continue on.

We had snacks on the bus back, but I completely shut down. I had eaten enough to be able to participate and now I couldn't do any more. I feel bad for doing this, though, because I should still keep my motivation up, and not give up like that. I shut down as well at tea. The nurses had warned me about becoming reliant on the tube, and now it was coming true. I figured that I was going to be fed anyway, so what was the point in eating and facing all the emotions that come with it? Eating is only there to keep you alive, and I don't want to be alive.

## Tuesday 14 August

We were going to the cinema today, and I felt so much pressure to complete my lunch. Was it really going to be worth it? Is it worth all the anxieties for a few hours watching a film? I didn't know, but I had to at least give myself the opportunity. I cried and cried the whole way through lunch. They were tears of frustration, fear, sorrow and pain.

We watched *Evan Almighty*. I had loads of emotions again about going out in public. What would people be thinking about my tube? Would they think that I was dying? It didn't look that dramatic, but that's what I wanted people to think, because that's what I want to happen.

We had to have afternoon snacks later than usual; I only managed a few dried apricots. I had decided before that I would only eat that much, and when I do this I absolutely can't eat any more because otherwise I will be punished by the voice, and I'd rather not eat anything than be bad and get punished.

After tea my key worker asked me whether I would rather try and make up my intake orally at eight o'clock or just get it tubed now. What a decision. Part of me enjoyed the tube, part of me hated the tube, part of me knew that I couldn't and wouldn't make it up at eight o'clock, but part of me wanted to try. I eventually decided that I would rather that it was just done now, because then it's over and done with. So that's what happened.

---

TEXT MESSAGE:
Everyone here in the village is thinking of you and is wishing you well. You don't realize what a beautiful person you are – just as you are. Of every young person I know, YOU are the one who can go out into the world, take it by the scruff of the neck, and do whatever you want to do and succeed. When you get yourself fit and strong again you can achieve anything you want. Hope you are back home very soon. xxx

---

## Wednesday 15 August

I had a really positive attitude today. I don't know what changed, but it was just there. I was going to eat everything and get the tube out. It was going really well until tea, but then the plate of food that came out in front of me was huge, it was too much.

The voice kept talking to me:

*'You can't do it. If you do eat it you know that I will punish you.'*

I cried and cried all through it, and when pudding came it just made it all worse because I had just climbed one mountain and now I would have to climb another one.

I finished, but I just had to get out of the dining room, and I locked myself in the toilet again. I didn't know what to do, I was being backed into a corner and suffocated by my feelings, I just wanted to scream, I was breathing quick, deep breaths and my heart was pounding, it felt like it was going to jump right out of my chest. I began to scratch at an area on my wrist until it was all red. I've never done anything like that before, but I was too lost and confused and I didn't know how else to help myself or let others help me. Punishment is what I need.

I spoke to my case manager[12] because she could see that I had been crying. She wondered what staff could do to help me after meals. I don't know though, I don't know anything. I know that I like to be alone, which is true. It gives me a chance to organize myself and drift away. She said that it often wasn't healthy to be on your own because you can often just get deeper into your negative thoughts. Especially when I feel so depressed and think that I don't deserve anything, I'm basically trying to fight a losing battle because my mind is just so one-sided. So we agreed that I could have my time on my own, but then I should go and discuss my thoughts with a staff member.

I carried on the evening feeling captured and bewildered by my thoughts and kept having small outbursts of tears. I'm due for my first review tomorrow. I keep wondering how it will go. I'm a bit scared – what are they going to say?

## Thursday 16 August

All my feelings came up after lunch, so I went out with one of the therapeutic care workers. We went out of the dining room and sat on the stairs. My feelings about killing myself were back and I couldn't control them. They prowled inside my head, and captured any last bit of hope that I had. She was going to talk to someone higher up, to discuss what to do because she said I needed more support in dealing with my feelings. I didn't want her to tell

---

[12] The case manager is the person in charge of your treatment plan.

31

anyone, though. I don't want to get help with my feelings, I don't want them to go away. I want them to stay and come true.

I also had my first review today. My parents and out-patient team came in and discussed my progress, and the best way forward for me.[13] They told me that they had talked about my tube, and making sure that there is good communication with my out-patient team. I asked how long I was going to be here. They said that they weren't sure, but I was ill enough to be in hospital at the moment, and I had another review in six weeks, so it was going to be at least till October.

I had family therapy[14] afterwards, which I think was really beneficial. We all sat there in silence at first, I didn't want to say what was bothering me, but I couldn't hold it in and I knew it had to be said.

'I'm sorry to my parents because every time I see them I feel angry, and I don't know what I can do to stop it, because I shouldn't feel it towards them, but it just comes. I know that it is partly because you are quite "lovey-dovey" and I just don't appreciate it. I know I should, but I can't accept it. Like on Saturday for example, I think we exchanged four hugs and kisses. This just wound me up because I'm so self-conscious about my body and I don't appreciate more physical things than necessary, and I would be more grateful for a quick good-bye. I want to prove my self-sufficiency and not to be oppressed by my parents.'

---

[13] The review meeting involves a member of the out-patient team along with the in-patient therapist, case manager, family therapist and hospital schoolteacher.

[14] Family therapy involves you and your parents, and sometimes other family members as well, talking with a therapist about issues to do with family relationships.

We then explored why I can't accept affection and talked about how sometimes we all need people to fall on in troubling times. Also, why I can't express my anger, and why I think that it is such a great sin. I think it's probably to do with the same connection that I have with 'thin = happiness' so that for me 'anger = bad'. I suppose I need to somehow change this thought process, but it seems so logical to me.

## Friday 17 August

Today started badly after I was told that I was back on observation for an hour after each meal, and after snacks as well if necessary.[15] I hate it. I don't want staff to be with me. I don't want them coming to the toilet with me to make sure I don't make myself sick, or do something even worse. I was so angry and upset that I couldn't face participating in the morning activity.

*'See, even THEY are punishing you now. They are doing this to you because you are talking to them.'*

It was true; I am now enraged by myself because if I hadn't shared any of my feelings then I wouldn't be in this situation. See, there's the proof that sharing negative feelings does mean that you get punished. I was already being crushed by my thoughts, and now the staff were crushing me too.

My coping method is starving myself, so for this reason my motivation to eat was totally cut off, and I didn't manage any snacks in the morning or afternoon, and had no fluids all day. For me, eating food is just another thing to worry about, another thing to bombard my head with.

---

[15] Being 'on observation' means that you have to have a member of staff with you at all times – either right next to you, or near enough for them to be able to see you.

In a key session[16] I had to go through magazines and cut out words or pictures which I felt related to me, or the way I feel, and then arrange them on a poster. Things I cut out included: 'weight-loss', 'size 0', 'size 8', 'In desperate need of help', and 'Out of control'. I found this really effective because without saying anything I was able to communicate, which I often find hard because I can't put my feelings into words.

After tea, the amount of Enlive I was due to have was so much that a plan was made to give it to me in two feeds. I was going to be given the first part now and then attempt to eat a snack, and then the night staff would feed me the second part – which would be even more if I didn't manage to eat the snack.

Even after the first 750 ml I felt really sick; it doesn't help that it is done quite quickly. After the second feed I felt so unbelievably ill. I explained to the member of staff that I felt like I was going to be sick, but she offered no support or comfort. As soon as I was off observation I went upstairs to bed. I reached the toilets and just threw up. One of the young people heard, and I asked her to go down and get a member of staff. They came up, but didn't do much. I tried to explain that it wasn't forced, but she didn't seem convinced. I'm going to sleep crying because my frustration is so huge, but I'm not going to go and get a staff member, I don't trust them and it seems pointless anyway.

---

[16] A key session is time with your key worker/s to do different activities, talk, share your feelings. They happen at least weekly, or whenever necessary.

## Wednesday 22 August

I had therapy today.[17] We mainly talked about my future because I was worried about it. One thing that I think triggered my worry was that the GCSE results are coming out tomorrow, and this for me brought out a lot of feelings around education. Would this illness ruin my chances of gaining all ten of my GCSEs next year? Would my school ask me to drop some? If they did, how would I feel? To be honest, I would be absolutely devastated. I feel so embarrassed that people don't think that I can cope. I would be letting myself and my family down. I have actually been thinking about my GCSEs since I was 11, and now they are just around the corner, but I am stuck in a hospital battling a mental illness and really struggling to see the point of living.

## Thursday 23 August

The GCSE results came out today, and it was really strange because they weren't even my results but I was nervous. I just kept thinking about what I will get, and how anorexia will affect my results next year.

The two young people in the group who had taken GCSEs this year got amazing results. One got 10 A*s, and the other 5 A*s and 5 As. I guess I feel jealous, because I'll never be able to gain such great grades. What I did find interesting, though, was that the young person who got 10 A*s said that she had worked and worked for those exams, to get what she thought would be a really solid start in life, but in actual fact it hardly

---

[17] This was individual therapy, which happened once a week, and was another place for each young person to talk one to one with a professional.

35

meant anything to her, because now she realized how much she had sacrificed her health for them. She forgot about her body and neglected it, and the things that mattered to her now were the small ones.

This was really mind-opening for me. I need to realize that life isn't measured by exam results – and perhaps I should stop thinking so far ahead, and just set small goals, like eating a meal, or not crying more than twice a day: just small things, but things that will hopefully give me a larger sense of achievement.

In my core team meeting it was agreed that my uncle and aunt could visit this weekend, which is a bank holiday. Also, the plan for how my tube is managed was changed. Up to now I've been getting ten minutes to make up the calories in Enlive after missing a meal or snacks; from now on I will have the chance to make up the missed calories in food at eight o'clock every evening. If I don't manage it then, it will be fed through the tube the next morning. The idea is to try to 'wean' me off the tube.

## Friday 24 August

The new plan for my tube came into practice today. I needed to eat two pieces of toast and a snack to get up to date. I just couldn't do it, though.

*'Why do you want to come off it? . . . It is symbolizing success . . . you are being a really good anorexic, and I am really proud of you for that.'*

So I went to bed knowing I would be fed first thing in the morning.

## Saturday 25 August

Mum and I went out to the local town when I had my visit. We went shopping and I picked up a top, but I couldn't fit into it. I found this hard, because I wasn't quite sure what to do with the fact that I couldn't get into it.

*'They did this to you.'*

It brought home to me that I have put on weight, and I find this hard to absorb.

## Monday 27 August

My uncle and aunt came today. It was great to see them and gave me a real confidence boost. We went bowling in the afternoon and had great fun. I didn't win, but I was surprised that I didn't take that out on myself, because I would usually take that as meaning I am a failure, even if it was just for fun, but I didn't, and it felt so liberating not to be pressured by my negative thoughts.

## Tuesday 28 August

We went back to Willen Lake today. We went on an orienteering course of 4 km. As soon as we were told this I thought about exercise, and it is still something very much at the forefront of my mind, because it is something that I have struggled with in the past. I was worried whether it would affect my weight.

We walked for about an hour and a half, and at the end I was so completely exhausted. My legs ached and I hardly knew how to move. I found this hard to deal with because it made me think about how much anorexia has taken away from me. I might have been exercising excessively before, but it meant at least that I had reached a certain level of fitness, and now not to have any of that made me really sad. I used to run 10 km, but now I couldn't even walk 4 km.

In the evening one of the other young people had a tube passed, and all my feelings just came rushing back. I feel sorry for her, but also jealous. I want to be the most ill. Even though having a tube passed is a horrific experience, I am proud of it. I am obeying my voice, and some day it will reward me for that – it told me so.

## Wednesday 29 August

In therapy we got talking about what achieving and what being the best actually means. In my life I have always striven to be the best, and where has it actually got me? I have turned my determination into something negative. I have used it to try and become the best anorexic. We wondered why I needed to drive myself to achieve so much. I guess it's because it is a way in which people can commend me, which I feel I need so that I can gain a confidence boost, because I can't find that self-belief. I need other people to appreciate me and my achievements because at the moment I am unable to appreciate myself and value myself for who I am.

## Thursday 30 August

The issue about my tube, and when it would be coming out, has been around quite a lot. I had to go for a meeting with my case manager after tea. She said that I should have a think about it before I went in.

When she asked me what I'd been thinking, I said, 'I think the whole "three day" thing is good, because once you manage to do this, it proves that you are ready to have it out, but for me, it just seems that it could go on for ever because as soon as I get to the third day I panic and stop eating. Maybe something like a set date would be more helpful, say Monday or Tuesday.'

'Well, how about tomorrow?'

There was then one of those very long, awkward silences.

I'm not ready to have it out. I don't want it to come out. It has become a part of me within less than three weeks. How could I say that, though? That I want another weekend of people outside looking at me, curious about what is wrong with me? I desperately want to disappear and become invisible – but I also want people to notice me, as I haven't got anything they can remember me by, only my tube. I tried a bit to explain this, but actually I don't want to because I am afraid that they might take it out even sooner. We came to the agreement, though, that it would come out on Monday morning, whether I was eating or not eating.

## Saturday 1 September

I rearranged my morning snacks so that it would allow time for me to go with Mum and Dad to Covent Garden in London and meet up with some friends there. It was really great, the healthy side of me realized that this was normal, and wanted to have a normal life, but I also wanted to have a tube in for the rest of my life. I can never escape this confusion.

On the way back a man offered me his seat on the Underground, I expect probably because of my tube. I didn't really think much about it at the time, except that he was a very generous man. However, in the car afterwards Dad said that it had brought a tear to his eye. I was quite shocked by this because although I was very, very grateful to the man who gave up his seat, I don't realize or understand how much my dad cares for me, and thinks about me. It doesn't make sense. I'm a person who has obviously caused him so much despondency, sorrow and frustration. Why should he care for me? I just don't get it. I am trying to think of reasons but I can't. All I hear is:

*'You are a failure, everyone hates you. Your dad is just pretending to like you. He is deceiving you.'*

I am sure that this isn't true, but I can't think of any reasons why it isn't true, so I just have to believe the voice.

## Sunday 2 September

I am really anxious about my tube coming out tomorrow, and I talked to my key worker about it. I am worried that I won't be able to cope, and that it will have to go back in. I also wanted to know whether it was going to be taken out before or after breakfast. I want it to be taken out after breakfast, because I think that I am going to find it really hard, so it will make it even harder to then be expected to eat a bowl of cereal. She agreed, and said that my request would be passed on.

I guess I'm so worried because I know that, as the voice keeps telling me,

*'It IS going back in.'*

I'm not ready. I'm not going to eat. I want to keep my tube. It's how I identify myself as a person.

## Monday 3 September

I sat down at the breakfast table, but then one of the nurses came to get me. I assumed that she was just going to confirm that my tube was coming out after breakfast, but she just said that it was coming out now. It ran through my mind to say something, but I was too scared.

Pulling it out was a lot quicker than putting it in, but no less uncomfortable. She said, 'Well, at least you have got your nostril back!'

I got up and smiled, but underneath I was crying a river, it was like a rainstorm was brewing up inside me, I could feel it all coming together.

I sat back down and my riverbank broke. I wasn't sure what to do with everything.

I feel that it was quite insensitive to take it out, because one of the reasons that I have become ill is because when I'm upset or angry, I take it out on food. I am also confused why my request hadn't been handed over, because as I predicted I found it hard. The voice just took over:

*'You're a failure because you don't look thin. You're not ill enough – just being in an in-patient hospital isn't enough. Having the tube gives you a status symbol, it tells people that you're not managing and that you are an anorexic – now, THAT is something to be proud of and hold on to. Keep going, my friend.'*

I do have another voice saying that I don't want to be ill, but it is nothing like as powerful, and I have given up trying to fight the negative one. Every day is such pure labour; it is like a thousand wars going on in my head each day.

I didn't manage any breakfast.

I am finding it so hard being off the tube. I am managing food, but I can't let myself drink. I feel like a swinging pendulum. The more I swing to the recovering side, the more the force pulls me back to the anorexic side. Therefore if I remain in the middle, I stay totally neutral and satisfy both voices. To me eating but not drinking seems like the perfect solution, I will be like a peacekeeper between the two sides.

41

## Tuesday 4 September

It was the first day of school today at the hospital.[18] I went through with my key teacher[19] how my timetable would be set out, and where I would do my extra subjects for GSCE (Geography, French, German and Latin). I was pleased because I've been really frightened that they might make me drop a subject.

In the third session of the day we were set some temporary maths to do, just until some work was sent through from my school. I suddenly felt really pressured again. I want to stay on top of my work because that is what I judge myself by, but I also know that my health comes first, whether it's positive or negative. The right balance seems blurred in my mind.

That evening during tea a nurse came in. I still hadn't drunk any fluids, and it had been two days now. I knew what she was going to do, and I really didn't want it to happen. She supported my head again because I was crying and kept moving it away. The tube came closer and closer to me, and was slowly pushed in.

It is corrupting me. It is my enemy but also my lifeline. It is unpleasant and sore, but offers my body fundamental nutrients to stay alive. It is a snake squeezing all the hope out of me and restricting me, forcing me down a disconsolate path from which I can't escape. I blame myself for everything.

---

[18] School time in hospital was about three hours a day, in which teachers would come in to teach maths, English and art – also dance for some. Different ages are taught together, but each person's work is supervised by an individual teacher.

[19] The key teacher is the hospital's contact with your school. She supervises how much school work comes through and how you are managing it, and guides you through reintegration into school life.

## Thursday 6 September

In my core team meeting I asked for consent to see either a friend or my grandparents this weekend. Although it would be less awkward seeing my grandparents with my tube, I think it will be more motivating to see a friend from school because it is them I am really missing. It was agreed, and because it was such a positive meeting I even managed half a glass of water at snacks.

I had family therapy in the evening. We discussed why I find it hard to talk to my parents about things. We wondered if it is because we are quite a jovial family, which therefore makes it hard for me to say if I'm feeling low for fear that I will bring down everyone else's moods too, and if I do that then I feel guilt-ridden and totally accountable for the unhappy mood. It was helpful for me to see that I can be sad, and that my parents will be able to cope with that – they are mature adults. Although I don't think that I'll be able to put this into practice.

## Friday 7 September

I spoke to my parents, but it was too late to arrange for a friend to come this weekend. I found this quite hard, because I had really built up my hopes, and I really believe that this is the motivation that I need to come off the tube permanently.

In the evening with my feed, everything just developed into a collection of uncontrollable emotions, and I couldn't deal with it. I tried to stand up and tug the tube out of the nurse's hand, but I couldn't and she kept on tubing my feed in. I pleaded with her through my tears to stop, but she didn't.

'Please, please stop . . . what if I don't want to live?' I screamed at her. She didn't respond.

I was put on observation again. I went out of the feeding room and tried to lock myself in the bathroom, but the nurse caught me too quickly. I was howling with frustration, completely distraught, and was trying to retaliate against her. I wanted her to leave me alone. I want to evaporate and be forgotten about. I was begging her to leave me alone. Another member of staff then came in and calmed me down. I don't really know why I went like that. I guess I am so frustrated with myself. I hate myself, and I hate this illness. It has captured me in its grasp, and it is never going to let me go. I'm better off dead.

## Saturday 8 September

My parents visited me today and everything was going really well until lunch. The agreement was that as long as I was up to date with food by lunch, whether orally or by tube, I could go out with my parents in the afternoon. After lunch I was down for a glass of Ribena and a glass of water. The nurse measured out 500 ml of water, we were about to go in for the feed, when another member of staff collared me and said that I had to be up to date with calories before I could go out, and therefore refused to let me be tubed the Ribena. So she made me go back for twenty-five minutes and sit until I drank the Ribena.

One side of me just wanted to drink it because I desperately wanted to go out with my parents, but the other wasn't sure whether four hours out was worth drinking it for, because it makes everything inside me so much worse. By choosing to drink I am taking sides, and disrupting my 'being neutral' plan.

I finally drank my Ribena, and then had the water tubed. My parents by now had now been waiting for well over half an hour.

When I came out to join them a torrent of tears streamed down my face and on to my dad and I was crying, 'It's not fair, it's just not fair!'

One thing that we had been working on in family therapy was that they should give me space to be able to say that I wasn't OK, and that I wasn't in the mood to be happy all the time. So in the car I explained why I was crying. It was a real breakthrough for me, and in the end we had a great time out, and it really helped me to see that persistence does pay off.

## Sunday 9 September

I spoke on the phone today to one of my greatest friends, who moved away in July. We just talked and gossiped about anything and everything! It really cheered me up. It was so incredible to talk, and it is one of those phone calls that I will never forget.

## Monday 10 September

In my key session we did something quite different. We went upstairs and used the drum kit to see if I could try and express myself that way. My key worker gave me different feelings or situations and I had to transfer these on to the drums. Examples included guilt, hope, the two voices in my head and depression. Things like guilt were large, strident sounds. Hope was very quiet, almost a non-existent tinkle. For depression there wasn't a noise. It was just a blank silence. It makes me feel empty inside. It hasn't got a beat or a melody. It's a continuous desolate space inside me.

It was really interesting and helpful, because it made me see which emotions are stronger and it was a different form of expression from trying to explain in words.

## Tuesday 11 September

In family therapy we talked about the death of my grandfather. For me, there has always been a great mystery behind it. I came to my own conclusion recently – that he died in our guest bedroom – but my mum always denied it.

He was staying with us because I wanted to show him my new junior school, so he had come down for a couple of nights. In the morning I was a bit surprised that he wasn't at breakfast and wondered why my other grandparents took me to school, but I didn't question it – I was only seven or eight at the time. In the afternoon when my parents picked me up from school they told me that Granddad had died that day on the way to the hospital in an ambulance.

In family therapy today I was told the truth – that he did actually die in his sleep in our guest room. Mum had found him dead in the morning, and she wanted to protect me, and didn't want me to see his body. Although it was hard to hear this, I am pleased that I finally know the truth and the reason for the redecoration of that room and the new bed. I totally understand why they did it, yet they still lied to me – and perhaps I am more resilient than they think? But why can't I be more resilient to anorexia?

## Wednesday 12 September

The issue around NG feeds was around quite a lot because there are now four people on NG tubes. Feeds can be quite distressing for some people and so it has to be done in the quiet room for safety. Even so, Enlive tends to get splattered around the walls and other members of the young people's group are quite annoyed about it, because the quiet room is supposed to be a place where you can go and just be calm, but when someone's in there being tubed it's not tranquil, and even if you go in there afterwards you can't be tranquil because you get a real sense of someone's pain, struggle and distress, which isn't at all comforting.

In Community Meeting[20] we talked about why four people were on the tube. I feel quite cross, though, because I was the only one of the four who spoke, and I'm not even one of the people who struggles or retaliates. Someone asked me why I felt I needed to be on a tube, and I replied, 'Because it is a way of punishing myself. I don't deserve to drink and nourish myself because I hate myself so much, everything about me.' I then started to cry.

I was upset for three reasons:

1. I felt guilty about being honest because I don't really want people to know what I had just said. I feel very exposed and vulnerable. I don't want people to understand my thoughts because I don't want to accept their help.
2. I was upset for feeling so bad about myself and don't understand *why* I just can't like myself. I'm too scared to envisage and dream about a future where I'm not ill, because I know that I'm never going to get to that paradise. I just have to accept that there is no hope.
3. I am also fed up with this stupid illness. They try and encourage you to talk about your feelings, but now I have done that, I actually feel worse. I want anorexia to leave me alone, but then again I don't want it to abandon me. I'm so confused about what I want.

---

[20] Community Meeting is the weekly meeting when everyone comes together to talk about issues affecting the community as a whole.

This evening, though, I found out that my friend is coming to see me at the weekend, which has made me so excited! However, this excitement is clouded by anorexia. I hate anorexia. It isn't an attention-seeking act. It isn't a faddy diet. It is a desperate cry for help. People outside don't understand. If I didn't have to go through this I wouldn't. I just want it to go away. I want the voice to stop talking – but it won't. It won't leave me alone.

## Friday 14 September

In the third part of Friday Group, one of the therapists said how courageous I was in sharing how I felt in Community Meeting, and how heartbreaking it was that I feel the need to punish myself. I didn't think about it much at the time, but during snacks I began to cry. I was still upset and frustrated with the illness. I want to move on but don't know how to. I guess I am also a tiny bit proud that someone has acknowledged how challenging, and what an important step, it was for me to expose my genuine feelings – and maybe because I feel proud, I don't know how to cope with that feeling, because I haven't felt that in such a long time. It was the most minuscule amount, but even so the non-deserving-guilt feeling seemed to come rushing back to me.

## Saturday 15 September

In the afternoon with my parents we went to a nearby city. The first place we visited was the cathedral. It was really beautiful, and it felt quite important for me to be there because I missed church last week, and I'm going to miss it tomorrow too. There was a board in the cathedral where people could write up their own prayers, and Mum wrote a prayer for all the staff in the unit, saying, 'May they protect and surround all the children with love and support.'

We then went into a beautiful park. I just loved being in such a wide open space, because I often feel quite confined being in hospital the whole time.

Next, we went to a museum. While we were there Dad and I built an arch out of foam bricks. It was really great to have a bit of a laugh with my dad, just playing and having some fun, because I think that he often feels a bit left out.

The only hard thing was when we were walking back through the park there was a cross-country run on. It made me think about what I'm missing out on and how much this illness is holding me back, but yet, why don't I want to let go of it?

I'm like a balloon, I'm all the air inside trying to get out, I'm pushing against the walls of the balloon, the anorexia. I just want to pop out and be free, but I'm not able to find the energy to pop the balloon and beat anorexia once and for all.

## Sunday 16 September

I was so excited that my friend was coming today, I just couldn't wait. When she walked through the door I just felt such a relief. We hugged and hugged and my eyes started to well up. I realized just how much I had missed her and everyone at school, and how much was being taken away from me by anorexia. I want to be free like her.

We just talked and talked and talked, and through one person I felt connected with everyone at school, and it reassured me that I wasn't being forgotten about. The laughter that we shared seemed to penetrate my sorrow and release all of the pain inside me.

Before she left we had a debrief with my key worker. We discussed how we thought the day had gone, and we all agreed that it had been really positive. My friend asked me how much I wanted her to say to people at school. I said that I don't mind how much she says because I just think that it is a fact – it's a reality – I am in an in-patient hospital with an NG tube. I would worry also that if people didn't know the truth then it would be exaggerated at school.

Saying goodbye was really hard, when we were hugging I just didn't want to let go. I didn't want to let go of this personification of hope, but I didn't cry because I was worried that the staff would then think that it is a bad idea for friends to visit me.

Despite this sadness within myself I managed lunch after my friend had gone, and I was able to stay up to date for the whole day. My friend represented hope and something clicked inside me. I didn't feel that I could eat for myself yet, but today I did it for my friends at home. I guess the next step is eating for myself, but that's only when I decide to believe that I deserve to nourish myself.

## Thursday 20 September

It was agreed in my core team meeting today that I could have two friends to visit me this weekend. I really believe that this is the motivation that I need to come off the tube.

---

TEXT MESSAGE:

Hi. I just want to let you know how worried me and my mum are. Really hope you are getting better. Just keep strong. I miss you so much. Everyone I know is so worried about you; we can't wait to see you when you are all ready and well. Love you so much. xxx

---

## Saturday 22 September

In the afternoon with my parents we went into the local town and as a treat I was allowed to go to a beauty salon. I had my hair cut and my nails painted.

I really do appreciate the treatments but I can't help but feel guilty. I feel like I don't deserve it. I know deep, deep, deep down that I do, but I need to work on trying to bring these thoughts to the surface.

## Sunday 23 September

My anticipation waiting for my friends to arrive was almost unbearable!

I was surprised, though, that I didn't feel very apprehensive about them seeing me with my tube. I think it's because last week it was all OK with my other friend. Even though I didn't feel too self-conscious with them, it was still strange because it's an anorexic status symbol, and I'm proud of this. My anorexia makes me feels good; it admires me and praises me for succeeding in being a good anorexic. It's a companion to me and a friend. It understands me better than anyone can because it's inside me. It always knows how I feel and how to resolve any of my imbalances. I'm so caught up within this powerful and overwhelming illness.

My friends brought a teddy bear which we named Hope. Also a card signed by the whole of my year. I really appreciate both of these because I do worry that people will have moved on at school when I eventually go back, and that they will have forgotten about me, but this really put my worries aside and reassured me.

When they left it was really, really hard because I wanted to try and stay positive because I had had such a good time. I had laughed and laughed and laughed, and I didn't want to let go of

51

that laughter and sense of fun, but it all just got too much and everything just seemed to escalate out of control and I went back to my coping mechanism of starvation. It wasn't just that they had left, it was other things as well. I was really cross with myself for still being on the tube. I wanted to be liberated, but the illness just won't let me go. As well as that, my periods returned at the start of this week. Although I am relieved, it symbolizes that I am putting on weight and getting healthier, which of course isn't what the voice wants, and it seems to be punishing me mentally for this:

*'This is what they are doing to you. They have put the weight on you that has made your periods start. You are following the people who are making you fat . . . why are you doing this?'*

My key worker decided to have an impromptu key session to talk about why I was so distressed. We both lay down on the grass and practised relaxation techniques such as listening to the wind and the leaves. It was good to try and unwind, however I couldn't stop crying for the rest of the day, and by the evening I was completely sobbing my eyes out. They are still bloodshot.

## Monday 24 September

After weighing this morning I was a bit worried because I knew that my out-patient team had set a weight for me to get to while I was seeing them before I was admitted to the unit, and I have now reached that, but I am still continuing to put on weight. I spoke to my key worker who reassured me that the weight gain wouldn't go on for ever, and I still wasn't at 100 per cent weight for height. The reassurance helped.

As well as getting reassurance from my key worker today, I also got support from my key teacher, because at the weekend a huge box of books from school arrived for me, and it was quite daunting because I am never going to be able to catch up on all of the work. She reminded me that my priority at the moment is my health, and the work will still be there when I'm better, whereas if I hadn't got help to deal with the anorexia then I probably wouldn't be here. It was helpful that someone else could put things into perspective for me.

## Tuesday 25 September

In my key session we went outside and practised 'how to get angry'. We started by whispering nursery rhymes, and then saying them, and then shouting. I found this exercise really hard, because somehow, in my exploration of emotions, shouting is classed as bad and negative feelings as things that shouldn't be expressed. Instead, I bury them further and further inside me – but now they've emerged as an eating disorder. Although I felt really uncomfortable, it helped me to start by realizing that it *is* OK to get irritated or upset. My key worker had to keep telling me not to smile, but it's just a natural reaction for me. When I feel out of my comfort zone or I'm scared I just push everything inside and conceal it by smiling, and I think that it's going to take a lot of practice to break this habit.

The most helpful part was when we pretended to play the two voices inside my head. My key worker was the healthy one and I was the anorexic one. We went through basically the battle that is continuously going on inside my mind every single day like a simultaneous role-play. It went something like this:

53

HEALTHY: Why can't I show my emotions?

ANOREXIA: *Because then you'll get better, you have to cover everything up, people don't want to know grumpy people.*

HEALTHY: People aren't always happy though, it's just not normal.

ANOREXIA: *Well, you're hardly normal, you're a complete loser.*

HEALTHY: I'm not; I know that I am not. You are just the deceitful voice inside me.

ANOREXIA: *No. I offered you so much, Constance. When you were standing on the edge of a cliff and no one was noticing you, I did, I saw your pain and loneliness. I gave you the opportunity to be thin, a great runner, goals to aim for, and I know that you love aims and challenges. I know you so well, I'm such a big part of you, and you would go back to being nothing without me. You'll be nothing if you let go. Nothing.*

HEALTHY: No, I would be healthy and have a life, and not have to be kept alive by a piece of plastic going into my stomach.

I found this exercise so helpful because I didn't think about how to phrase it, it all just came out, and it is my true battle. I'm sitting here crying now as I am writing this down because every day is such a continuous battle and struggle with such a split mind, and the anorexic voice seems to have an answer for everything. What was good to know was that my key worker was saying the same things that I say to myself. It was reassuring to know that if someone was in my shoes then they would be saying the same opposing things.

I don't know whether it was the key session or the fact that I didn't want to be fed, but I managed all my fluids today, and I seemed to handle the consequential thoughts much better, which I suppose is a big achievement.

## Wednesday 26 September

In therapy we talked about how I would feel if I had to give up a GCSE, and I almost can't bear to think about it. The embarrassment would be intolerable. I have an expectation of myself. My parents, the staff and my friends say that they don't have one, but I don't believe them. I would feel so ashamed that I couldn't cope. I personally think that it would have the opposite effect if I was made to drop a GCSE because I would feel that I would need to compensate and work even harder on the other nine, and therefore just get into the cycle again of work becoming an obsession. I cried about this. I don't want to be more of a failure than I already am. Failure is a catastrophic event for me – and I just seem to fail at everything I attempt – that's why sometimes I don't know why I attempt to do things because I know what the outcome will be. When I fail it feels like I am falling into a bottomless black pit within myself, and all my attempts seem to wither up inside me. People say that I haven't failed – but I don't believe them. They all say I am a 'high achiever', but that just puts more pressure on me. I guess that I have learnt to cry though since I have been here, and realize that it is OK. I just haven't reached that stage yet with anger.

## Thursday 27 September

I had family therapy today with my grandparents as well. It was great to see them, but the first thing that my grandma said was,

'How lovely it is to see you. You look so beautiful and so well.'

I found this hard to hear because I know that I am really not beautiful, and I also found it interesting that she thought that I looked well when I had an NG tube up my nose! – I guess a different take on it!

We talked about the past and how my grandparents looked after me for quite a long time while my parents were both working full-time. We discussed how our family is like an upside-down pyramid. I'm the only person of my generation, so it's like I am supporting the rest of the family, which could put me in a hard situation, because I feel that if I do something wrong, then the rest of the family will crumble.

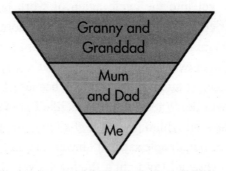

*My 'upside-down family pyramid'*

Grandma also used the expression that I am the 'jewel in the crown'. I think that this just shows what the family thinks of me, and that increases the expectations that I have. A jewel in the crown is never bad, and also is always polished. I have to live up to that expectation.

Altogether it was a good session and I think that we all learnt a lot.

## Friday 28 September

I had a review today. It was decided that the treatment programme will continue whether I have the tube or not. I am quite pleased about this because the tube is acting as a complete block against making progress – so long as I have it in, I can't have meals with my parents, let alone go home at weekends.

After my review, my parents and I had a meeting with my key teacher to talk about my GCSEs and future education. My teacher was concerned that trying to do ten GCSEs while still having anorexia would be too much, and, knowing that I would accept nothing less than A* grades, she was worried that it would put my recovery back. She suggested that we just bounced ideas around the room. Mum went first. She said that she would be quite happy and delighted if I turned round and said that I would only do five. Dad then said that he wouldn't be bothered if I said I wanted to drop everything and go surfing for a year, and then do some GCSEs when I felt ready. I obviously wasn't too happy and got quite emotional about it. I just can't understand what they are talking about. Here's why:

1. Only three years ago I had a tutor to help me prepare for my 11+ exam and scholarships.
2. I don't think asking me to drop something will help, because

I'm just going to have to compensate for it and so I will work even harder on the others.

3. I would be too ashamed to go back to my friends at school and say that I have had to drop some GCSEs. It would be just too unbearable. I will have let myself down, and also all my friends.

4. I gain my self-confidence from three things: sport, thinness and academia. I'm not allowed to do sport for the time being, and I am never going to be allowed to become thin, so therefore academia is my only thing that I have to define myself; if that is taken away then I would just feel like my life was even more out of control, and then there would actually be nothing to live for.

My teacher then suggested moving schools. This also was not going to happen in my mind. Even if I was too ashamed to face my friends, and parts of the school such as the toilets would bring back memories, I know that it is the best school for me, and it has offered me so much support.

At the end of the meeting I could hardly bear to even look at my parents, I was so cross with them. I just stood there like a statue while they put their arms around me and hugged me goodbye. I wonder how the visit will go when they come again tomorrow, and whether I am still going to be angry.

## Saturday 29 September

When Mum and Dad arrived I seemed to forget about the day before and just got on with my visit as normal. In the afternoon we went to an RAF museum. While we were there, one of the guides asked me what the tube was for. I felt really awkward because I didn't really know how to answer or even if I wanted to answer at all. Mum stepped in, though, and just said:

'She hasn't been very well lately, and has just come out of hospital for the afternoon.'

It was left at that, but it was still quite a peculiar situation because I have never been confronted by a stranger about the tube before. Although I was embarrassed, part of me craved the attention and was delighted that someone had noticed me and that I was ill. I just want it to end, my anorexia or my life, either one will do, but right now I would rather have the latter. The misery that is caused by this unspoken voice is what I deserve.

After the museum we went into town and I was bought a ring which is hopefully going to help me get off the tube. I will wear it, and it is to symbolize that I am struggling, rather than having to have a tube to show it.

In the evening I read an article in the newspaper about how you can inherit anorexia. There was the mother's story and then the daughter's story. The final line of the mother's was '. . . and I've just learnt to cope with my anorexia.' This hit home really hard for me and I am quite daunted by the thought that anorexia will never leave. Does that mean that I will just have to 'cope' with it? Just for example, at my wedding will I not be able to have a slice of wedding cake because I will be too worried about the calories? Will I never wear a bikini because I wouldn't want people to see my figure? The word 'cope' denotes struggle for me.

## Monday 1 October

Today was quite good because I was told that my level of observation had been reduced, and I wasn't on observation after meals anymore. I was pleased because I'm not going to act on any of my really powerful thoughts any more. Although I'm still struggling to see the benefits of getting better, at least now I don't want to take my own life.

---

TEXT MESSAGE:

We all love you so much and please remember that – please. All I want is for you to get better. School is OK – would be tons better if you were here though! I miss you more than a kid misses its toy. All my love. xxx

---

## Tuesday 2 October

I had a really good phone call with my parents tonight. It feels like real progress to have a positive phone call. We talked about how I find it more comfortable to know that my friends know the truth, which came up when my friend visited me, because I think that her knowing has stopped any rumours. Perhaps being honest doesn't work for everyone, but for me it is the best thing because I have found out who my friends are, and instead of living a double life, I've found out how much support people radiate out of themselves for other people in times of need, and these rays of support have really helped me.

Mum also said that some people were upset that I hadn't invited them to see me, and we discussed why. I realized that these particular people were really close friends who I had known for a really long time, and I would feel too embarrassed for them to see me so ill. But right now I just needed their continual support, which I wouldn't have received if I hadn't been honest about my anorexia, so I wanted them to know about it even if I wasn't ready to see them.

## Wednesday 3 October

Before Morning Meeting[21] a member of staff came in and said that there was a dying plant or something in my bedroom. I knew that I had a flower arrangement, so I went up to check if it was mine.

Bits of it looked dried up and so it didn't look very attractive any more, but it was absolutely fine otherwise, and it certainly didn't smell. I threw it away anyway even though I didn't want to. I felt really guilty because my granny had made it for me and so I felt quite sentimental towards it. It was even harder because I am particularly worried about her at the moment: I think she is very lonely, and earlier in the week she sent me a letter saying that she was sorry for making me ill. I just feel so awful that she is blaming herself for my anorexia, because of course it wasn't her – life has just thrown its own curve in for me. Throwing a plant away might seem quite an innocent thing, but it just accentuated my concerns.

I had a meeting with my key teacher at noon. She was worried about my neatness in presentation of my work, and that it might be one of my anorexic habits. To be honest I am pretty cross because I believe that I am just a naturally neat person, that is just who I am, and in the grand scale of things right now, I think it is quite insignificant. Also, because being neat is who I am, I feel that if I tried to be less neat it would be contradicting the main thrust of

---

[21] Morning Meeting is a daily meeting of the community at which everyone has a chance to say personally what was helpful and unhelpful about the previous day.

the work that goes on in the unit, because it is all about expressing who you really are, and so by covering my neatness up, and making things messy, I would be going against that principle.

The whole morning just seemed too much. I was upset and confused and I didn't want to express any of my emotions openly. I took a giant step backwards at lunch and didn't eat anything. I was a cannonball dropping further and further back into my dark and deceitful thoughts.

*'Don't eat, Constance – you know that it will make all of these troubles go away.'*

This evening at snacks, for the first time in ages, I felt hungry, and my stomach hurt. Something must have clicked with me. It brought back all the memories of being hungry, the collapsing, and at that moment during evening snacks I realized that I don't want to live like this. This small sensation of hope really pulled me through and enabled me to make up my calories for the day. I just kept thinking of the future and what I want to achieve.

## Thursday 4 October

I have really struggled with connections with the rest of the young people this week. I have felt an angry vibe from them. I have felt really isolated and lonely, and today especially I didn't speak to one young person. I've really drawn back into my shell.

My separation from the rest of the group continued and I didn't want to talk about it with my parents and we had a very short and awkward conversation, and now I feel so awful for being direct and saying that I didn't want to talk to them. I am lost and now I have pushed away the two people who could have offered comfort and security. I do love them both so much. I am a terrible person.

## Friday 5 October

I felt really attacked in Friday Group today because quite a few of the young people were cross that I didn't eat any of my lunch and this was hard to hear.

I want people to like me, but it seems that I have to eat in order for people to like me, and I can't let myself do that yet. I'm so terribly lonely. I really want to go home, but I know that I can't survive at home and work with my difficulties. I don't belong anywhere.

Another thing that made my day harder was that I was allocated to two therapeutic care workers,[22] but I had no check-ins or catch-ups with either of them during the day. This just added to my feeling of loneliness, it's like nobody really wants or cares for me. I feel a bit like a stray leaf blowing in the wind, going whichever way the wind, or my thoughts, take me, without having the support of staff who act as my branches holding me down and stopping me from getting too caught up in my thoughts. I really need those strong branches right now.

---

TEXT MESSAGE:

Hi darling! How are you? I haven't spoken to you in ages and I miss you. I'm in English hiding behind my book! Lol! Tee Hee! Love you. xxx

---

[22] Therapeutic care workers are the staff who take care of you during the day, although they are not directly connected with your care plan.

## Saturday 6 October

I had a supervised meal[23] with Mum and Dad today. Beforehand we had a talk with my key worker in which we talked about any worries that were around. These were mine:

1. I knew that I had to eat everything in order to be able to go out with my parents in the afternoon, but just because I eat everything I don't want my parents to think that everything is OK. I am still ill, and I want people to know that.

2. I didn't want to find it all too overwhelming and break down in tears because I didn't want my parents to see me cry. I don't want to be weak.

My mum didn't seem to have too many worries because I guess that she has seen it all – the ups and downs of when I have been at home. The times when I was able to push through the negative thoughts and eat – and the times when I was too weak to even stand up without collapsing.

However, Dad was quite concerned because this was the first time in about five months that he had seen me eat – at home, Mum would usually try to give me dinner before he got home from work at night.

Both my parents wanted to know what they could do to make it easier, and I wanted just to talk about normal things, like what a normal family would talk about over lunch.

---

[23] A 'supervised meal' is a meal with your family/parents and a member of staff in the dining room. This is then followed at a later stage by an unsupervised meal, which is just your parents and you.

The meal itself was really hard. The voice was really powerful and I found myself needing to struggle more. The voice was telling me that I couldn't just put a mask over it and pretend everything was OK. I had to look like I was struggling, every mouthful had to be slow and forced. Having this meal was such a big step, and a step to getting rid of anorexia, but it seemed to hold on to me even tighter now, determined not to let me get out of its clasp.

If I had disobeyed then I would have upset my only true friend – it may be deceitful but when I work with it then it makes me feel so good and powerful and nothing can replace that. If I upset it then I must be a really, really bad person.

## Sunday 7 October

I only went to church for half of the service today because it was the harvest festival and to be honest I don't really want to go to church to celebrate food. Before it started, though, one of the congregation, who I see every week, came up to me and said:

'My grandson was anorexic, but is coming to lunch today and he's got through it, and he has just finished university, so just keep going and you'll get there too like him.'

I got complete goosebumps all over. It was a very short conversation but her words were just so inspiring and touched something deep down inside me and shone a light on me for the rest of the day.

I spoke to one of my friends on the phone in the afternoon and she also offered words of inspiration and support. It reminded me what support was out there for me and today I feel like I actually want to get better, which in itself is a revelation.

## Monday 8 October

In Monday Group[24] we played 'Human Bop-it' and 'Honey I Love You' and I have never laughed so much in my life, I was actually crying with laughter!!! Then, during tea one of the therapeutic care workers said that she didn't know that I had such a giggly and bubbly personality. I thought about this quite a lot, because I wondered why this was, and tried to think of reasons and all I came up with was because my mind is so corrupt and it does really drag you down deeper and deeper so it becomes increasingly more difficult to be positive and smile.

In the evening I received the most amazing text from a friend which meant the world to me and it felt like hope would never end. It read:

---

TEXT MESSAGE:

I'm friends with Constance because she's really cute and funny and when she smiles it makes me feel good inside. I'm comfortable around her and don't have to try. She's kind and considerate to other people's feelings.

---

I'm going to finish today with that.

## Wednesday 10 October

I had a key session today and I was told that the tube had to be changed and was going to be taken out on Monday at 6.30 p.m. which left me with very mixed feelings.

---

[24] Monday Group is a get-together for the young people and staff in the afternoon to have some fun, for example playing group games.

I am going round in a bit of a circle. Again I'm not ready to have the tube out, but will I ever be ready? Every day that it stays in, I feel more and more reliant on it, and it has been two months now since the first one was put in, and I've had one in for the whole time except for a couple of days in the middle. I know this isn't the life I want to lead, but if I let go, then I'm bound to punishment by my mind, and giving in is by far the easiest option.

In the evening I made a list of the pros and cons of drinking. It did help me to put things into perspective but my worries and concerns about the tube coming out haven't seemed to budge.

## Thursday 11 October

In Creative Group[25] the young people had to suggest something that others in the group could do, something which was outside their comfort zone. For me it was suggested that I do something more 3D and try and incorporate my feelings into it, because I don't tend to express them that much.

I made a heart-shaped box with a slit in the top. I then wrote my worries and concerns on a piece of paper and posted it through. I then decorated it with glitter. It was a step, because I was expressing my feelings, but I still didn't feel ready to share them with anyone else. Covering the box in glitter also seemed quite symbolic, although I didn't think about it at the time, because I often disguise my feelings and mask them over, a bit like the glitter was hiding the misery of those thoughts inside.

---

[25] Creative Group meets every fortnight and gives you somewhere to be creative and express yourself through art.

11th October 2007

- The tube is coming out on Monday. I'm not ready, but will I ever be? I'm scared that it will have to be inserted again. If it is, am I just setting myself up to be here forever?

- I hate myself, everything about me, especially my body image, and everytime I eat it just gets worse. Will it ever stop?

- I haven't made any progress, and I've been here 3 months - HELP ME!..

- The young people don't seem to like me at the moment :(

*My thoughts from inside the box*

68

I had family therapy afterwards which felt really helpful, because we talked about our family dynamics more and how we are so sensitive individually.

My school was brought up too, by my dad. He explained quite bluntly about the reality of me being here. They have already paid lots of money for a school term that I am not even at. In an ideal world, he wanted me to be back on 5 January when everyone goes back. This really seemed to strike a chord with me. I am fully aware about the money issue involved, but it seemed to mean more because someone had talked about it directly. This experience also helped me to see how beneficial talking directly can be.

In the evening I was told that I would have to have my supervised meal with my parents on Sunday rather than Saturday, but Dad wasn't able to do this, so this is going to have to be discussed tomorrow.

## Friday 12 October

In Friday Group, splits and divides among the young people were discussed and how certain members of the group were being left out, and my name was mentioned. It was suggested that I am 'bobbing below the surface'. Personally, though, I feel more like a baby bird flapping its wings on the edge of the nest, but just not being ready yet to take that leap out of the security that I know. It feels too scary right now.

After the group, I was told that I couldn't have a supervised meal this weekend because the unit can't do Saturday and my parents can't do Sunday. This brought feelings up that I seemed to be open about. Some were my own, genuine feelings, and some were my anorexia's. I was angry, but actually more frustrated because there weren't enough staff. But anorexia has twisted this into the fact that I am not worth enough to people for them to let me have a supervised meal. More importantly, I was also upset because I had really been doing a lot of thinking about how Mum, Dad and I can improve and move forward from the last meal, so that I go from using the staff's support to using the support of my parents in an unsupervised meal. So I therefore felt quite let down.

## Saturday 13 October
In the afternoon we decided to go to Hay's Galleria in London but the Tube was shut, so we had to drive to the nearby town and get the train, which was always going to be tight, because I didn't finish my feed until 2 p.m. I could feel the stress rising, especially from Dad, and for the first time I was able to confront him about it. It was scary, because I didn't want to upset him, but afterwards I really felt the benefits from being open with him and he said it was only because he wanted me to have the best and longest afternoon out in London possible. The rest of the day went smoothly and it was a giant leap that I had taken.

## Sunday 14 October
In my key session I made three different-coloured bracelets:

- a green one, signifying anger and frustration;
- a blue one, signifying feeling low, upset or anxious;
- a gold one, signifying confusion, questions or that I need to talk to someone.

They are in preparation for my NG tube coming out tomorrow. The idea is that I will wear the one that matches what I am feeling so that my allocated member of staff can recognize what I am feeling and help me with it. They will allow me to receive help in the best form and not take me too much out of my comfort zone. If I could just try and get some of these emotions out, then I wouldn't need to express them over food, so then I won't have to have the tube back.

## Monday 15 October

I got some feedback from school on some work that I had sent in. This felt really good, because it helped to reassure me that people weren't moving on while I was away and that I was still being thought about.

At 6.30 p.m. it was time for the tube to be removed and my key worker came in. The mixed feelings seemed even more powerful now. It felt like my armour and protection was being taken away. I would now have to fight without it; I couldn't blame things on having a tube, and I would have to express myself, which I didn't feel ready to do. I've used it as a bit of a scapegoat. I hate the way I look, my body, my face, but with the tube in I could blame that, because without it, then perhaps I would be able to see myself as a prettier person.

I am cross that it had to be taken out, but now that it has gone I feel upset. But I feel glad, too, because this is an opportunity to show what I can accomplish – yet it also seems like just another opportunity to fail.

I talked to my key worker about my problems with connections. I talked, for the first time, about a really good friend who moved abroad in the summer and how much I miss her. When others at school used to confront me head-on about eating and exercise, she would be there to talk and be more subtle about it. She used to be an ear to listen to my problems and a shoulder to cry on at school when it all became too much. My key worker wondered whether anorexia really took control when my friend left, and suggested that perhaps I struggle in making connections with people because I'm afraid that they will leave again. I found this talk really helpful because it feels like we have really got to the bottom of at least one of my problems.

## Tuesday 16 October

The morning started off well: I didn't want the tube to go back. But as the day went on, I felt that motivation slip right through my fingers.

In Feelings Group,[26] it was mentioned that it had been quite a big day for the community because two people have had their tubes removed. I was invited to talk about how I was going to express myself now. I became very anxious and I felt very reluctant. I explained about the bracelets despite not wanting to.

*'You can't tell people,'* it told me.

I went against it, but consequently felt so awful and guilty. I feel exposed and vulnerable now people know what I am feeling by looking at the colour of the bracelet. If I don't wear one, it means that I am OK. I took it off in Feelings Group because I felt so self-conscious.

---

[26] Feelings Group is a group that meets weekly where you can express your feelings with the other young people.

I think part of the problem lies in time. I can't understand why people would want to give their time to help me – I'm just worthless. I haven't done anything really wrong, so I can't really explain what I've done which makes me hate myself so much. I think that is why it is so hard to unlock, because there is actually no real answer or reason – it is just a very strong voice.

After Feelings Group I had some time to think and I put my blue bracelet back on. I was able to realize that, although it is still hard to know that people know what I am feeling, ultimately it is helpful. The staff congratulated me because they saw it as a real improvement – I, however, do not.

## Wednesday 17 October

I had therapy today. It was the first session I had had in about two months when I hadn't had a tube in. It felt quite strange and really exposing. We talked about my feelings around it, and I was able to talk more openly about it. I can really see the benefits of not having a tube. I can see how much of a block it is. For the first time since it has come out, I feel really free and liberated, and this feels really good.

## Thursday 18 October

I was still a long way behind on my fluids and I really didn't want to go to my core team meeting because I knew how the conversation would go – it would end with them passing the tube for the third time. My core team meeting was at 2.30 p.m., and my mum was picking me up at the same time to go to the orthodontist because my retainer had broken and it was the only time he could see me. We were just about to leave, but they called me in, and of course it came up – but they came up with three ideas about passing the tube, if I continued to be low on fluids:

1. The tube would be re-passed as normal.
2. The tube would be inserted, but I would have to feed myself through the tube.
3. The tube would be passed at a particular time during each day, every day if I wasn't up to date. After each feed, it would then be taken out.

I don't want any of those, especially not the third one.

I got into the car with my mum after the core team meeting and burst into tears. I can't believe that I am in this situation again. I can't bear the thought of having a tube passed again, but I can't see another way out.

I DON'T WANT TO DRINK – I DESERVE AND WANT TO DIE.

I arrived at the orthodontist still crying, and this brought on a whole new set of worries. I found it hard to trust the lady because I didn't know her. I think the roots of the trust issues that I have stem from my relationship with my mum, because I often still blame where I am now on her. I begged her not to tell anyone about my not eating and drinking, but she did, so now I don't trust anyone. People ALWAYS let you down. As well as that, the bill was a lot of money, which could have been spent on something much more important than me, and I feel terribly guilty.

When I returned to the unit, I was told that if I continued not to drink, then they would pass a tube tomorrow and I would have to feed myself.

## Friday 19 October

My key worker fetched me from lessons at 10.30 a.m. and told me that I was going to be tubed at 10.45. Of course I didn't want it, but I missed the tube, I wanted it back as my friend.

I started shaking when they were inserting it and I totally tensed up. I kept groaning through my mouth as I could feel the cold plastic scraping down my throat. This time, the process seemed much more brutal, and my nose started bleeding. I felt like the brutality must be a punishment. I didn't like feeding myself, but as it was my first time the nurse did most of it for me.

In the afternoon a package came for me. I opened it eagerly and it was a signed poster from the teenage pro-surfer Bethany Hamilton in Hawaii saying: 'Constance, never give up.' Someone gave me her book about her journey after she got her arm bitten off in a shark attack, and I found her story truly inspirational because of her dedication and faith. However, I am truly confused about how she knew I was here, and how the parcel got to me. Later in the day I found out that my mum had got in contact with her. It was such a big boost for me. It is hope.

---

TEXT MESSAGE:
Awww Connie that is so cute! You are so strong and I am so so so proud of you. Please do not stop believing that you can do it – because you can. We all have faith in you. xxx

---

## Saturday 20 October

My visit from Mum and Dad started well until we got on to talking about the school athletics trip to Lanzarote which I signed up for a year ago. They thought that it would put too much pressure on me to expect me to go in six months' time, but I feel like it is going to be a real motivation for me. This then moved on to an argument about trust, and how I didn't feel that my parents trusted me because they thought if I exercised and lost weight then that would be because of anorexia. They can't understand that I didn't do well at running because I sat back and relaxed. I trained, and I love running and it is a real passion for me. It is like a fog has covered over the logical side of my thinking, and what was worst was that Dad had got tickets to the rugby World Cup today and he gave them up to see me. This made it all worse because I also feel guilty. He would have had a much better time at the rugby, and I should have come second. I eventually walked out of the room – I had had enough, I hate disagreeing, and this was really the first time that I had ever done it with my parents.

I talked to my key worker outside. She was pleased that I had shown my emotions and stuck to my opinion, especially because it was different from my parents'. It is apparently a real step, but it doesn't make it any easier. I believe that if I show any negative emotion then people will hate me, because I am not being 'The Perfect Girl'. As I am writing, I can see that it doesn't make sense and sounds so illogical and of course it isn't true, but it sounds so real in my head.

My key worker went back in with me and we talked about it. Mum got quite upset because she couldn't believe how shallow and 'black and white' my thinking is. This just made me more upset because it is just another thing wrong with me. I HATE MYSELF, I have so many BAD qualities. I always ask myself: 'Why do people support me?' I've written a list of why people shouldn't like me and why I don't like myself. Here is a list of what is wrong:

1. The weight that I've put on.
2. I'm really ugly.
3. I'm really stupid and I get loads of things wrong at school.
4. I have a really unattractive shaped body.
5. I can't trust people so they shouldn't like me.
6. My personality is really bland and uninteresting.
7. I don't look nice in any clothes.
8. I have no confidence and never laugh.
9. My thinking is obviously very shallow.

With all these true reasons, why on earth do people like me? They must be pretending.

## Sunday 21 October

I had an amazing time when one of my friends from school visited me today. It was great to catch up and feel included back at school. I definitely think that it is easier to stay up to date when you are happier in yourself. It was a really positive visit.

## Monday 22 October

I had case management and we talked about the tube – it will come out next Monday. We also talked about the Lanzarote trip. Yes, I can see why people are concerned about letting me go. I would have to be in control of my eating and exercising, and they wouldn't know if I started making myself sick again. But it still frustrates me – will I ever be trusted . . .?

## Tuesday 23 October

I was thinking a lot about the tube today. I love all the attention that I get from it, I want to prove that I am an ANOREXIC and I am SO PROUD of that, but on the other hand I just want to escape into a small hole and never to return, after all, it can't be any darker than the place that I am now, and it would be far easier.

## Wednesday 24 October

We had an Egyptian-style buffet today. I was pleased with how it went, because it was definitely easier than the first one, at the start of the summer, when I just broke down in tears. The thought of having to choose and eat my own food frightened me so much. I could see an improvement this time, even though improvement is such a negative word to me.

In my therapy we talked about the changes that I was experiencing in myself. I could feel very subtle changes, a bit like I was slowly being turned 180°. Half-term has provided me with quite a few reality checks. Many of my friends have been away and meeting up – it has shown me how much I am missing out on. Seeing them helps with this, so I don't feel so isolated, but it is also heartbreaking to know what they are going home to at the end of the day – a free life, without an inner god dictating to them and destroying them.

I am feeling more confident that this time, when the tube comes out on Monday it won't go back in because of this new motivation that I have discovered, and I pray that it will continue.

I was thinking a lot about prayer today. I pray every night to

God, although I never pray to Him to make me better. Instead, I ask that He helps me to make the right decisions on the road to recovery.

I believe that He chose this path for me, so I should continue it and try and work with it, with Him holding my hand all the way, a bit like that bit of my favourite poem, 'Footprints in the Sand':

> The Lord replied,
> 'The times when you have seen
> only one set of footprints in the sand,
> is when I carried you.'

Perhaps it was chosen for me because He knows that I am going to be a stronger person when I come out of this tunnel, perhaps, I don't know, but no one can stop me from believing this. This is one thing that anorexia cannot take from me.

## Thursday 25 October

I continued to feel really motivated today as someone was discharged. Before, when people have been discharged, I've often felt quite low because I just think that it will never be me, but today I actually felt like that could be me one day, and that was a complete revelation, a very new feeling – belief.

## Friday 26 October

I am trying SO hard at the moment, I have eaten and drunk all my meal plan for the last few days, and today I really noticed how not eating affects other young people, as this time I was on the receiving end. This really helped me because I became slightly cross with the young people who weren't eating, so therefore they are 'bad' and I don't want to be bad, so I must eat, so strangely my 'black and white' thought processes seem to have worked to my advantage today.

## Saturday 27 October

I had a supervised meal today with Mum and Dad, and I think that it went really well. What helped was that it was with the same member of staff that I was with yesterday, so we were able to talk about it yesterday and the continuity felt really helpful. As this was my third supervised meal the staff member took more of a back seat, which also helped because it was seen as an improvement.

In the evening one of the young people gave me a ring that she had bought for me to wish me good luck for when my tube comes out on Monday. It was so cute, and it felt really special that a young person really cared about me, and was thinking about me – it gave me hope.

## Sunday 28 October

Lunch was really difficult today because one of the young people was refusing to eat. For me and another young person this completely blew it and we both couldn't deal with it. A special meeting was held afterwards, so we could all try and get our feelings out which felt really good because I have so many mixed feelings. I have a huge day tomorrow, my tube is coming out, and I have so many voices in my head all saying not to eat and the temptation to become reliant on a tube again just gets a thousand times worse. Although today felt so hard, this meal did feel like such a big turning point because I was able to see myself that I can overcome really difficult times, and actually be proud of myself. I realized where not eating gets you – nowhere – and I don't want to be in that place.

## Monday 29 October

Following on from yesterday, I was able to eat tea, even though I was so petrified about my tube coming out. It came out after tea and my key worker came to hold my hand while it was taken out. It felt comforting that someone I have a really close connection with was there, because it was a really hard moment as well as a very big one. I had been preparing for this mentally for a while, and now I feel like I will never have an NG tube again. Never. Today I have faced my future.

## Tuesday 30 October

Nothing really happened today. I'm just trying to stay focused on what I want, and what I need to do. I am just blocking out everyone else's struggles and realizing that I want my life back, and believing that I have a great future ahead of me which I can't achieve with anorexia, because anorexia is no future for anyone.

---

TEXT MESSAGE:

I went to St David's today and prayed for God to give you strength and courage. It's not anorexia that makes you special. It makes you deaf and blind to the love and friendship that was always there for you, and always will be. xxx

---

## Wednesday 31 October

We had our Halloween party tonight. It was just great that all the young people could come together as a community and have fun and forget all of our individual struggles.

## Thursday 1 November

In my core team meeting I asked for an unsupervised meal and snacks out this weekend and I was given them, which I was really pleased about, because I am reaping the benefits of eating, and not looking back.

I have also now reached a healthy weight so they proposed two possible options:

1. Reduce my meal plan.
2. Start introducing exercise to my plan.

I was pleased about the thought of doing exercise because it is something that I really enjoy doing, and I want to learn to do it in a healthy way again, and especially while I have support around me.

However, introducing exercise can't happen for a little while, because it has to be arranged, so for the time being my meal plan is going to be reduced.

## Friday 2 November

I felt really guilty today because in Friday Group I started a conversation about how unhelpful comments were being made by some of the young people to other young people, and they were quite upsetting. They were things such as 'Why is she still here . . . she is really fat,' or 'Move your fat arse.' I feel that this is inappropriate language to use anywhere, let alone in an eating disorders unit, because on the very rare occasions when I do look in the mirror I *do* see someone who is fat, so it is absolutely soul-destroying when someone says it to you, even if they don't realize the impact that it has on you. Also, it isn't about the food and weight, these are just the physical symptoms; it is the inability to express yourself. This is where people get it so wrong.

I don't know whether it was the right thing to do, especially because I am still racked with guilt, but I guess that I can only learn from experience, and realize that just because I vent some of my feelings it doesn't mean that I am a horrible, horrible person.

## Saturday 3 November

My parents' visit started off quite rocky because I came out to meet them and my mum said,

'You seem a bit quiet?'

I found this annoying and unhelpful because of the way that she assumed that I wasn't OK, without giving me the chance to say that maybe I wasn't feeling that great today, and I was hurt by this. I was able to say that, though, and as a family we were able to get on with the visit. I can see that this might seem like an insignificant incident to some people, but it means a lot to me, and I think that as a family we can really learn from these experiences which can help us in the future, perhaps with bigger issues.

Our unsupervised meal went really well. I was able to use the support of my parents, which was really great and such big progress from two or three months ago when I didn't even want my parents to see me eat. I feel proud of this milestone that I have passed today and it helps me to see what I can achieve with determination and persistence.

## Sunday 4 November

It was the monthly trip out this Sunday, and what with church as well, I was really worried. I thought that it was going to be quite a challenging day.

In church, it was the first time that people had seen me without a tube, and some people did take a double look, which brought back my feelings of exposure.

The outing was really hard because, for one, I don't like being in public places because I don't like people looking at me and making assumptions, such as how fat I am and weight-related presumptions. Also, the only two young people who went were myself and one other who is thinner than me, and I don't like being the fattest person. I can't be the fattest person.

It is really difficult to unstitch all my feelings around body image. My thought processes are like a woven blanket, and I need to unpick every stitch to reveal the real me. I know that I have said before how my world is very black and white. You are thin or fat, a healthy-looking person doesn't exist in my world, and part of why I don't like going out in public is because my eye always turns to thin people, and that is who I compare myself with.

Before we set off on the outing I was able to talk about these anxieties with a member of staff, and together we came up with a plan to help me. While I was out, I was to try to incorporate a third person into my scale – a healthy-looking person – and to recognize these people. This definitely opened my mind and really challenged how I thought, which was really good. I was able to recognize two healthy-looking people while I was out, and she praised me for that. It may only have been two people, but this was a really big thing for me.

## Monday 5 November

I had a meeting with my key teacher today about my GCSEs. Although I was still quite edgy about it, she was pleased that I was able to think about the option of giving up a GCSE. In the past, whenever the subject was mentioned, I would just shut down and cry, and totally dismiss the idea, because academic performance is how I identify myself. I have realized that a compromise has to be made between taking five and ten subjects. I have learnt to trust my key teacher, and realize that she won't make the decision for me, she will just guide me into making the right decision which will ultimately be the best for my health.

I also had a key session today and we talked about body image which I found quite hard, because it is quite a sensitive subject. I explained how I basically live in a world without mirrors, because I know that the image that I see reflected back is one showing the misery that I am living in, the self-hatred, my twisted and toxic thoughts, and it is an image that I don't want to be reminded of. It is easier not to look in mirrors or see my reflection in glass because of what those images symbolize.

I try and try and try to make myself look nice, but however hard I try, I can never please my inner voice which controls me, my efforts are always in vain, and I can't imagine a time when I will ever be truly pleased with how I look, and I don't dare to think about it, because surely this can only lead to disappointment . . .?

I spoke to one of my friends tonight on the phone, which really cheered me up. I find it so reassuring to have a strong friendship with someone who I know doesn't judge me for where I am. Having a phone call is really motivating because my friends believe that I can get better, even if I am not able to hold on to that dream yet.

## Tuesday 6 November

I had another talk with my key worker about body image today. One of the incidents that had happened to do with body image was when Mum had asked if I would like new underwear, and I said no purely because I knew that I would have to see myself in just underwear and right now that is too hard.

The same applies for swimming. There is a swimming trip every other week, but I am just too scared to go and face up to the real me. I don't let myself see myself properly, and the thought of other people seeing me before I even know myself is too uncomfortable for me. However, I decided to think about the idea of going one week.

## Wednesday 7 November

Today was awful. Before Morning Meeting we were all brought together and told that one of the young people had taken an overdose and was going to A&E. A torrent of thoughts flooded my mind. How could this happen? Was it my fault? Was it something that I had said? Was she trying to commit suicide? The most powerful thought of all was concern. This young person has become a really close friend and what if she dies?

I was so proud of her, because she was able to tell staff what she had done, but it scared me to think what was going through her mind, because it had seemed like such an ordinary morning. I have never experienced anything like this before. Although I have seriously thought about trying to kill myself in the past when I have just felt too low and helpless to carry on, it would take a lot for me to act on it, and I can understand why my friend did it – it is what anorexia makes you do.

It is scary to think this has happened because I have the image of this hospital as a sanctuary that can protect you from the outside world until you are ready to face it, a safe environment for all us young people to work on all our struggles and difficulties – but this has made me realize that it isn't, and bad things can and do happen.

A special meeting was held later in the day to say that the young person was going to be OK, which was such a huge relief for the whole community. Many things had to be rearranged during the day, and the staff were surprised about the lack of anger coming from us. I think, though, when someone is hurt, it blocks out all other feelings and you can only worry until you know that they are safe, and I don't think that this is something to get angry with them about – it was obviously a huge cry for help.

Along with that, there was also a new admission today who was on the tube, which brought up some really hard feelings about the past for me. It is really difficult to see someone else on the tube because I am still so tempted to go back and become reliant on it again, so today it was really hard to keep strong and focus on my own recovery. I hope that I never have to experience a similar day.

## Thursday 8 November

I had a school meeting today with my key teacher and my parents which I was really worried about because I had a vision of it being the same as last time.

To be fair, it was nowhere near as bad, but it did leave me in quite a low mood. I find it really hard to talk about, because my school work means so much to me. It is like they are removing my harness which keeps me safe. Without it, I will have to understand myself, and there is going to be a period, until I discover the real me, when I won't have a harness to keep me safe, but right now I don't feel ready to take the leap and let go – I don't know how or where to begin.

## Friday 9 November

Nothing particularly happened today, but after snacks some people started to go home[27] and it reminded me that it could be me next weekend!

## Saturday 10 November

It was my day out today. We had a pre-trip talk. I felt quite patronized by my mum because she was worrying about what she should do if I didn't eat. I am in a totally different mind frame now and whereas before if something was wrong I just wouldn't eat, I can now recognize when I am finding it harder and I am prepared to talk this through, and try to rationalize my thoughts. I felt like she was expecting it to go wrong, which wasn't helpful for me.

Lunch was made a bit harder because we went to the Science Museum in London, and the tables there are long, so we were on the same table as other families and I felt quite exposed by this, but I said this and my parents were able to help me by focusing on the fact that the other people probably weren't taking any notice of us. This was really good. In fact, the worst part of the day was when Dad fell asleep and started snoring in the Imax cinema – how embarrassing!!!

---

[27] A visit home is the next stage after going out with parents for the afternoon. It had been mentioned in a core team meeting that I might soon be ready for this.

Overall the day was really successful and really positive and I am able to see what I have achieved, which I know is going to help me to keep focused and persist on this journey.

## Sunday 11 November

I saw one of my friends from school today which was really good. I think one reason why it is so helpful is because while I'm in an in-patient unit, it is much easier and tempting to compare myself (especially in size) with the other young people because we all have eating disorders. With my friends, though, I don't, because they aren't ill, so I am able to stop myself from comparing. We took loads of photos of each other and had loads of fun. It was the first time, though, that one of my friends had seen me without a tube. This was positive, but it still made me crave the tube, because I want people to know that I am still ill, and I can see that when I get this thought in my head, this is when it all goes spiralling out of control, but I can't stop it, I can't, it always comes for me.

I became very worried when my friend said that people at school were worried about another person who is showing 'anorexic behaviours'. I can't explain how it makes you feel, and I am going to sleep tonight crying on my own. God, I feel so alone. Isolated in my head. Trapped. I am worried and scared for my friend; I wouldn't want this entrapment for any one of my friends. I don't want anyone to go through the pain and struggle that I have to endure every day. I also feel cross. Jealous. This is MY illness and I don't want to share it. Anorexia gives me a power, a gift that only a few people have. It makes me feel special and unique; it found me when I was lost. IT IS MINE, and mine ALONE.

## Monday 12 November

I had case management today and I was told that I was probably going home next weekend, and I could start exercising in a few weeks. Although this was such great news, images of the past came flying back to haunt me, and still, still the illness seems so tempting . . .

## Tuesday 13 November

I had a meeting with my key teacher today. I wanted to show her the work that I had received from my school and she wanted to tell me two things.

One was that she had spoken to my school and she was going to visit it and have a meeting either next Tuesday or the one after that. I then suggested that I would find it helpful to attend too, and she said that she would think about it.

The second thing was that a deadline would need to be set for my GCSE choices. The date would be confirmed after the meeting. Overall it was a really good meeting, especially the way she praised me for my progress and that I was really considering doing nine GCSEs instead of ten.

## Wednesday 14 November

In therapy today we really focused on my beliefs around size. Why exactly do I see myself as so unattractive? It was really helpful to do this, and think of some counter-arguments in my black-and-white mind. Being able to recognize a healthy size is really helpful and so is telling myself to STOP when I can feel myself comparing.

Anorexia is a noose that just gets tighter and tighter around your mind, restricting your opinions and views. I can't help thinking, though, that it will never completely loosen, and that I will always be restricted.

## Thursday 15 November

It was decided today in my core team that I would go home and stay over for a night this weekend – I'm soooooo excited!!!!

## Friday 16 November

I was of course pretty nervous about going home today, but also really excited.

I realized how much I should appreciate things. For example, we were stuck in a traffic jam on the way home, and while Mum was getting cross I was absolutely loving it, because I hadn't seen one in four months – it was the same with street lamps, and I had forgotten my favourite radio station and my toothpaste when I got home was all dried up.

We saw my grandparents. Because we hadn't told them that I was coming home, when we had almost reached their house Mum stopped the car and I got in the boot. Mum then went in to get them saying that she needed some help getting some things out of the boot of the car, and so Granddad opened it up and there I was! To be honest I think they were more shocked to see me than anything!!! It was really fun though!

My first meal went surprisingly well. But I couldn't help but notice that the level of support dropped, which I did find hard. In the evening, we played Scrabble as a family which was really good, because it felt like there were three members in our family again – the fourth member, anorexia, had gone.

## Saturday 17 November
In the morning, we went to the local town and then we came back and did a puzzle. What I noticed was how different meals were. In hospital everything is weighed, but here we just did it by eye, which feels really liberating.

In the afternoon, I met up with some friends from school which was really good and we all walked along the canal. I was pleased that they treated me as normal, although part of me did want them to realize that I was still an ill anorexic.

I was quite upset when I got back to the hospital at the end of the afternoon because now I've had a taste of home I don't want to let it go. I have seen my future and it feels good.

## Sunday 18 November
Nothing happened today. It was incredibly dull!

## Monday 19 November
In the evening one of the other young people and I were mucking around with our phones and recording ourselves singing. It felt really good to have a laugh and a giggle together, because it doesn't happen very often.

## Tuesday 20 November
I think that today I unconsciously made an effort to speak my mind, and I do feel a lot better for it.

The first time was in Morning Meeting when I said that it was unhelpful that we weren't told about a new member of staff joining because I worry about what they think of me. The second was in Feelings Group, when I said that I felt helpless towards one of the other young people, whom I really want to try to help but don't know how to. The third was at the table during tea when I told a member of staff my opinion about a young person who was struggling. I realized this evening that it is OK to say what I think, and no one is going to die from it, nothing truly catastrophic is going to happen.

In the evening my phone call home was quite upsetting because I felt confused and overwhelmed by what I was feeling. I am fed up with being in hospital, yet I know that I need to be here. I feel very vulnerable to my own thoughts and I am craving protection, which I just don't feel that I am getting at the moment. I want to be wrapped up in a blanket and to have all negative things blocked out, but I am already wrapped up and smothered by a blanket of anorexia. I am taking that leap from the security of anorexia. I am in the transition period when I have seen the future but I am too scared of it. Right now I am between anorexia and health and I am not feeling like I have an identity or any protection.

## Wednesday 21 November
In the evening, when I was in the shower room, I caught a glimpse of myself in the mirror in just my pyjamas and I spontaneously burst into tears. I have such major issues with my body, and I feel so alone and ashamed of myself for being so fat. I am FAT, UGLY and a piece of NOTHING.

## Thursday 22 November
We had family therapy today and we covered various topics. One of them was how we can support each other – how I could give feedback about what is helpful and unhelpful and how my parents

can then learn from that. The therapist described it as a dance, where I have to lead and show my parents, and they follow.

We also discussed my self-doubt. I often say something but then doubt myself and regret it. I step out of the box, but then retreat into it again. We decided the way to combat this habit is for my parents to remind me when I do this.

## Friday 23 November

I had my review today. It was decided that the balance owing for the school trip to Lanzarote would be paid to enable me to go. I am not denying the situation that I am in, and I know that it will be a big challenge. I know it will be, but I think that it is going to be such a big incentive for me. It was also decided that at Christmas I'll probably have two shorter times at home. I can start exercising, and hopefully a discharge date will be some time in late February. It was such a positive review, but yet it all just felt so soon. I wanted to say STOP, but I couldn't.

*'This is it. This is your opportunity, get out of here as quick as you can and then you can do what you want,'* the voice was telling me. Was this really my opportunity to slip back into my old ways?

My first reaction was to stop drinking, but I now know that this won't get me anywhere, and I spoke to my case manager because I became really upset at lunch. She guessed that I might have found the review a bit much. It was reassuring to know that my recovery process would go at my pace, not theirs, and certainly not my anorexia's pace. Reassurance was all I needed. As a result of the reassurance, I was able to combat the anorexia by saying that this is not an opportunity to slip back – this is an opportunity to get my life back.

## Saturday 24 November

I'm at home for the weekend again, and today I did some exercise for the first time in about six months. I was of course a bit worried because I didn't want this to be a trigger, so that it becomes an obsessive trait again. It was good doing it again. I feel that I am in a position where I can manage it. I was in the gym with a one-to-one coach, so I felt connected in a safe way, and in a secure environment. It opened my eyes to a new kind of exercise, because I have never been to a gym before. I realized that I could get fit without having to go on long runs on my own.

I have such bad memories of exercise. I would go because I had to, not because I wanted to. I couldn't say no. I even had to go out in the snow once. I was so cold, freezing, but I had to keep going. The icy air whipped against my face and my whole body shivered, but I had to keep going.

This afternoon I went to my school and watched some rugby matches. Although I wanted to see some people, I was very nervous, and I felt really vulnerable. How would they know that I am still ill? I am not thin any more and I haven't got a tube. I still want to be ill. I tried to push this thought away, but it is so tempting, and this voice always recurs.

We had dinner with my aunt and uncle. Once again I was in the same dilemma. This is what I need to do to get better, but how will they know that I am still hurting inside? My main feeling for today was vulnerability.

## Sunday 25 November

Lunch was hard because we hadn't decided on a pudding, which was unhelpful, because I like to know what I am expected to eat, so that I am prepared. I managed the pudding, but afterwards Mum said to me, 'Are you proud of yourself?'

I didn't really know how to answer. I wanted to be, I really did, but it is like I can't let myself because that is bad, because I am fighting against my inner voice. It forbids all things positive.

## Monday 26 November

I had a key session today which was very reflective. I wrote what being well and being ill meant. This is my list of answers:

*Being well*
- freedom
- choice
- school/family and friends
- vulnerability
- acknowledgement

*Being ill*
- a sense of achievement
- protection
- security
- self-esteem boost
- acknowledgement

'Acknowledgement' is in both lists because I feel that I get it in two different ways. One will be in admiration because I will have overcome one of the hardest things, and the other will be from my anorexia in appreciation of my struggles. Which one do I prefer, though? Part of anorexia is that it becomes a secure world to be in. It is like a rock, and as I move further towards health, I drift further away from this rock. I need to find another one because at the moment I feel I am just bobbing around in a huge sea waiting for someone to rescue me. So we also came up with possible rocks for me. They included Mum, Dad, friends, sport (in a healthy way) and my out-patient team. I just have to wait until I find the right rock, which may not even be one of these but something different.

## Tuesday 27 November

In my school meeting I was able to hear the views of my school if I give up some GCSEs. This decision just feels so huge. I am starting to understand now that it is totally unrealistic to try to catch up on so much work after missing so much school, and I still don't even know when I am going to go back yet. I was able to hear their opinions, and they were able to hear what GCSEs mean to me – security, self-esteem, a chance to prove myself and a sense of achievement (however, not as great as anorexia).

Afterwards, I saw some of my friends. I was really worried about seeing them because of this recurring feeling of 'How will they know I'm ill?' I don't think I really tackled this feeling, partly because I don't know how; instead I just pushed it away for the time being and concentrated on the support of my friends and how much they seem to value me.

## Wednesday 28 November

Following my meeting yesterday I made my GCSE choice today. I am going to drop Geography and Latin, because these are the two subjects in which I haven't been sent any work yet. This feels like such a big step because I am moving away from the security, the self-esteem, the chance to prove myself and the sense of achievement that I get from school work.

## Thursday 29 November

I just found today that many things got to me, and that I was really alone. The signposts were there, offering the right direction to help, but I couldn't, and didn't want to, take it. I had been going in a steady horizontal line, but today each little thing just seemed to send me a step lower.

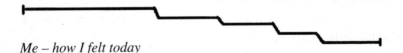

*Me – how I felt today*

## Friday 30 November

I got home and I was making Christmas cards downstairs and my parents were disagreeing about redecorating my room. They are doing it as a 'well done' gift for when I hopefully get discharged, and a motivation for me in the meantime. I felt really sensitive about it, like it was all my fault. I just sat there pretending that I couldn't hear anything even though my head was spinning with overwhelming guilt. I guess that it is just one of those situations that you can only experience at home, so it is probably going to be useful.

## Saturday 1 December

I went to a party tonight with my parents. I was really anxious about going because I still had the thought about 'How will they know that I am ill?' When I got there, though, I enjoyed it and really valued the normality of the evening.

## Sunday 2 December

I had lunch with a friend today. It was very hard, but I think that it helped because my friend got to see that I am not better and I still have major issues with food. I am able to see how far I have come, although I am still not ready to be proud of myself yet. I can see how I have picked myself up from being rock bottom, without a glimmer of hope, to where I am now, and that does feel good, and even anorexia can't deny me that.

## Monday 3 December

I made the connection today that I won't have left hospital before Christmas, and I think for the first time I actually regretted my past. I am frustrated by why it took me so long to want to get better. Although I have made this realization, being ill is still attractive, but it is starting to drift away like a fledgling bird that had made its nest inside me and it is now beginning to leave its home.

## Tuesday 4 December

I found out today that my first key worker is going to leave in January. It was really hard for me to hear. I had to keep telling myself that it is not my fault, she is just moving on, but I couldn't help it; however hard I tried to convince myself, it felt like another thing that I had done wrong, and that I am just being abandoned and forgotten about. I have finally learnt to open up to someone, I have shared my deepest inner thoughts with her, and now she is leaving. I would have liked for her to stay until my discharge because then she could really value my recovery, and understand all the hurdles that I have faced and conquered.

## Wednesday 5 December

It has been one of those days when everything just seems to catch up and start to snowball in my thoughts. My key worker is leaving, comments were made about me, and I couldn't help doubting myself about my GCSE choice.

I have made the wrong decision, and now I am going to have to live with that for two years. I like Latin, I like the challenge; did I only drop it to please other people? By making me drop GCSEs it feels like they are insulting my intelligence. Where is my motivation to go back to school, if I am going to be ashamed to be there? Nothing seems fair.

When so many things are spinning around in your head, eating gets harder and your body image gets worse. Once again I find myself fat, ugly and worthless.

## Thursday 6 December

I had family therapy today with just Mum. We talked about Dad, and how although 99 per cent of the time he is the most lovely and caring person, occasionally he does have a bit of a short fuse, and how I find that it affects me. To me, arguing is bad and shouldn't be done. When Mum and Dad started disagreeing at the weekend, it automatically sent me into a downhill spiral of thought processes.

'Oh my goodness, is this happening the whole time? Is this going to be the last one? Is one of them going to walk out? Where will I go for Christmas?'

I don't know whether I can't distinguish between serious arguments and minor disagreements because I've been at boarding school so I have never really experienced them, or whether I am just incredibly sensitive. I think, though, that with more time at home I will learn to be able to tell one from the other, and realize that disagreements, even arguments, are quite normal within a healthy relationship.

## Friday 7 December

One of my school friends came over, ate with me and then stayed the night. I really valued the evening because it felt so normal, and I was able to forget all of my difficulties and just be a normal teenager.

## Saturday 8 December

Mum and I went to the local town today, which seemed like a really good idea. However, I truly underestimated how hard I still find it to be in public places. People can't see the struggles going on underneath the surface. I became very self-conscious and didn't know how to get away from it. I wanted to retreat into my illness and hide away within myself again.

## Sunday 9 December

In handover today when I came back from my visit home, Dad said to my key worker that 'Saturday's tea was effortless'. I was really shocked by this and it really affected me. I love my dad so much, but if he thinks that a single meal is ever effortless then he is clearly mistaken. Eating is ALWAYS hard, it just depends how I manage it. It made me think, 'Do I need to show you that I am not managing? What do you want me to do to show you that it is hard? . . . Stop drinking? . . . Go on the tube? . . .'

However, as soon as he'd said it, he realized exactly what he had done. All the same, as a consequence I found tea hard. Who could I express myself to? I just had to battle this strong urge and realize that I KNOW that I am struggling, even if other people seem not to understand.

## Monday 10 December

My case manager gave me two possible discharge dates today. This felt really helpful, something to motivate me. They were 14 or 28 February. I guess that I am leaning towards the 14th because I have said to myself all along that I don't want to be in hospital on my birthday (which is in late February).

## Tuesday 11 December

We had the hospital's Christmas Day today, because of different people's annual leave. It was really good to have fun and to laugh – especially at the Staff Christmas Play – a rendition of *Aladdin*! It really did mean a lot, as I do find it hard to laugh and enjoy my life.

## Wednesday 12 December

I went to homework club tonight. I just got such a boost from working and achieving something. I really miss feeling good about myself. I know that gaining it from my work isn't good or healthy, but right now I don't know where else to get it from. I am in a barren desert and I am searching for any resources that I can find, and academic work seemed like an easy option.

## Thursday 13 December

A decision has to be made by tomorrow about my discharge date. Part of me is so excited about this, but the other side is absolutely scared stiff about having to re-enter the world after being protected for so long, first in my illness, and then in the hospital. How am I going to manage? If the 14th is my discharge date, then that is only eight weeks away, and this seems even more daunting. I have now stepped through a door – the door to recovery. Deep down I know that this side is more rewarding, but anorexia still isn't ready to let go of me. It's like a magnet not letting me go more than a certain distance away, and drawing me back to it. How can I reduce the pull of this magnet? I just don't know, and will I ever be able to do it enough in eight weeks?

## Friday 14 December

Before I went home Mum and I met with my case manager which wasn't a great success even though the 14th was finalized as my discharge date.

Before we went in, Mum said out in the corridor, 'We're just going to talk about your discharge.' This threw me into a complete panic because I don't want people to know about it, because then there is going to be a huge expectation on me, and we know from the past that this really isn't helpful for me.

## Saturday 15 December

For the first time today I was able to drink some water while exercising. It was only 50 ml, which I know is absolutely nothing, but it was a start, and a real breakthrough. As well as that I also had an extra 100 ml today, which was also great because I find it hard to nourish myself. I could feel the anorexia getting stronger because I was violating it, but I just kept thinking that it was what I needed to do and a great step to getting better.

## Sunday 16 December

During afternoon snacks I was talking to my friend on the phone in my room and so I had my snacks unsupervised. It was really cool because it was spontaneous. Of course, the thought of hiding the food somewhere did enter my mind, but I didn't, and to be honest I was too preoccupied with talking, and I felt pleased that I was stronger than my anorexia.

## Monday 17 December

Today felt really productive. I talked to my key teacher and, hopefully, I can have one day at school on 14 January.

I also spoke to my case manager. I asked whether it would be necessary for me to have a new key worker as I am leaving only a month after she leaves. I also talked about my weight, because I am still gaining weight every time I am weighed even though I am meant to be on a maintaining diet. I am becoming even more self-conscious about whether you can see this extra weight. She said both points I'd raised would be discussed in a staff meeting.

## Tuesday 18 December

Nothing happened today . . . very dull!!!

## Wednesday 19 December

I caught myself in the mirror again this evening and I am truly ashamed at what I see, all I can think about is how THEY made me fat, and that is how I am always going to be, fat and ugly, and I'll never be able to lose it because people will start to worry again. I have completely blocked out all the positives of how far I have come and of being healthy. I start to cry alone in my room . . .

To Constance

HAPPY christmas
and
happy new year!
Thank you for my card, it is really good!
I like the name Emily for the bear!
I am so so so proud of you, I could never
say that
to many        *May the Christmas*
times.
I miss you    *Season bring you*
so much,
It was       *happiness and Joy!*
really good to see you the other day!
I love you so much, you're doing so well,
Stay strong and keep going! we're all
here for you and love you so so so
much! I can't wait for you to come
back I miss you so much! We're all late
to lessons now!

I          I love you lots + lots
♥             from
∪

XXX

*A Christmas letter from one of my friends*

105

## Thursday 20 December

Today started badly after weighing. I have continued to put on weight despite being on a maintaining diet. I just got back into bed and cried. It isn't fair! Why am I STILL putting on weight? I asked to talk to my allocated worker for the day before breakfast because all the thoughts of not eating came back, because I didn't know how else to control my weight or my feelings. But I did manage to eat breakfast and the rest of the day improved.

## Friday 21 December

Before the first part of my leave, I was given my Christmas pack from my key workers which included some really beautiful and meaningful words. Reading these words made me feel confident that I would conquer this weekend.

## Sunday 23 December

I saw a friend today which was really good and she was the first person I told that I was going to come back to school in January. It feels good because I can look back on all of my achievements so far, but I also get a great sense of vulnerability because it is such a big world out there, and as my world starts to get bigger, my network of support gets smaller. I also have so many bad and painful memories of being at school, such as excessive exercising, collapsing, making myself sick, and hiding food. I am scared about having to face these again, and going back to the place where I was so deceived by anorexia, and so deceitful to my friends.

Dear Constance,

Hi there doll, hope you are doing ok over this Christmas time.

Be kind to yourself and realize that your emotions may be going a bit up and down during this time. At Christmas there a lot of people around and you may feel some expectation to perform and your parents may be a bit stressed and say things that may be a bit insensitive. This is just because they are probably a bit worried and want to make things 'happy' over this time. Try not to take them too seriously!

Now remember that you are always welcome to call for a chat to staff at [redacted]. You have the rota of who is here on which day. I would prefer you to call and ask for help instead of really feeling horrible and alone. So do not hesitate to call!!!

Now remember you ROCK and are a GREAT gal and this time of celebration and excess will soon be over. If you are not in the mood to celebrate remember be KIND to yourself- you have been at [redacted] for a while and it is your first long stretch at home. So take it easy and remember it may not be a smooth ride but we will have some information about where the wobbles still are and things you still need to work on before discharge.

Heaps of love and kisses
[redacted] xxxxxxxxxxxx

*The wonderful letter my key workers wrote me at Christmas*

## Monday 24 December

Every year, we meet up with family friends and have dinner with them on Christmas Eve, but I had loads of anxieties this time and questions surrounding it. I didn't know whether the sons of the family should know or not, because in the past I have been very open about my anorexia, and I don't mind people knowing. This is why:

1. I hate lying – I'd much rather people know the truth.
2. If I don't say anything, I will imagine that rumours will start, which would be much worse, and probably exaggerated from the truth.
3. *I am proud of my illness, and I want people to recognize me, if for nothing else, for being an anorexic.*

What I learnt today was that I don't need to tell people about my illness and that the urge for people to know is slowly wearing off.

## Tuesday 25 December

This Christmas is definitely more valued for two reasons:

1. The fact that I am at home which is great.
2. How today was as normal as possible, and my illness didn't get in the way.

From my parents I got a bracelet with the Lord's Prayer written around it which felt really special, because I think that I have definitely used Him quite a lot during this journey, and I feel more connected with Him now that I have this bracelet, because it feels like He is with me always.

## Wednesday 26 December

Coming back to hospital on Boxing Day was hard. There was something so special about being at home and being normal, and my time with my family has given me a huge insight into what my life can be like when I am better and home.

I am at the stage where I am ready to move on from anorexia, and I really want to, but it is so hard to come back to a place full of NG tubes and underweight people. It is a constant reminder of my past, from which I now greatly want to move on.

## Thursday 27 December

Weighing: I had lost quite a bit over my time at home. I hadn't done anything extra on purpose to lose any, but I can't help being really proud, especially as it wasn't on purpose – that just makes the pride even greater.

## Friday 28 December

When Mum and Dad picked me up from hospital today we went to Wales for a weekend treat, which was so exciting, and gave me a real boost of confidence, because it is a place that I love to be.

However, it does bring up some hard memories because it was the first place where I tried to make myself sick. I failed the first time, but I still went consciously into the bathroom with that intention, and that emotion and strong urge is something that I don't want to remember. It is that voice that tells you that you HAVE to do this. There is no way out, and you can't ignore it. You know deep down somewhere inside your mixed-up mind that it is wrong, but you just can't understand how or why.

## Saturday 29 December
We did absolutely nothing today. It was really nice to relax!

## Sunday 30 December
In order to go surfing, I had to eat an extra snack. I say 'had to' but I guess that I didn't have to, which then gets on to the question, 'Who am I actually doing this for?' Am I doing this for myself, or for other people? I often think that I am doing it for other people just to get a quiet life almost. If I do eat then people don't seem to interrogate me so much. However, in the back of my head I DO know that I am doing this for myself, because I have seen glimpses of my future at home, and it is these glimpses that I have to grab and hold on to.

Surfing was great. I loved every second of it, and I forgot every single one of my difficulties, which is such an uplifting experience. Lunch afterwards was hard, though, everything seemed to catch up with me. I didn't like the thought that people could see me in a tight wet-suit, I felt so self-conscious. My parents also seemed to be very tense, which didn't help me, and their tension transmitted through to me, making me feel very uncomfortable. I also had a huge guilt from eating the extra snack.

I can't put the two and two together yet, which is that if you do exercise you burn calories so by eating extra you aren't gaining any more weight, you are just making up for the lost calories. I can understand it in principle, but something about it just doesn't seem right in my brain. Extra food very much equals extra fat. I also felt that I had more food on my plate than my parents.

I just sat there and stared at this plate of food and the more I stared at it the bigger it seemed to get, and the task became even more daunting. At first I said to Mum and Dad that the problem was that I had a bigger portion. As the minutes passed, though, I lowered my very anorexic, defensive barrier and together we realized that it wasn't really about the portion size, but about all those other things which had unbalanced me.

This was quite an interesting experience because I got to see the power and effectiveness of expressing your feelings and how communicating and talking DOES WORK.

## Monday 31 December

We were meant to be going to a New Year's Eve party, but once again it all just got too much like yesterday and an explosion of fears and emotions came out. It was like an exact repeat of yesterday. A black cloud covers up your mind, and all of your rational thinking. It actually feels like something is compressing your head, it's almost physical. You are aware of it, and can acknowledge it, after all it has been your friend, but as soon as it re-emerges, you become so lost and unaware of your real emotions that it just takes over everything.

I put up my wall of protection, my anorexic barrier – everyone is trying to make me fat, you don't understand, etc. Mum stayed very calm during this moment of vulnerability, but was stern with me, which was really great. It was the perfect combination between empathy and strong positive reinforcement. Her words were,

'Yes, you have put on weight, but that is because you've been admitted to hospital with starvation, and you would have died if you continued to lose weight.'

I felt a sudden change; I turned on my light of truth and pushed away my wall. It was protecting me from all my other feelings, which I learnt from yesterday are far more real and truthful, and this other load of crap that anorexia tells me is all rubbish!

My truthful feelings were that I didn't want to celebrate something that I didn't want to happen. The new year of 2008 signifies moving on into the unknown, reaching out further into the world. Being at school in two weeks, being discharged in six weeks – can I really manage it all? Am I ready? People won't understand that I am still ill, I'm recovering, but still ill because it is not about appearance any more. There are also anxieties about school. I haven't got my uniform yet, what if I don't fit in?

Today was another example when talking helped, and I realized that it was the underlying things that mattered. We didn't go to the party.

## Tuesday 1 January

I wouldn't be lying if I said that we did nothing, because we didn't do anything I just flopped in front of the television, watched films, did a puzzle, and tried to be hopeful about 2008.

## Wednesday 2 January

Back at the unit today I had a handover with my case manager, which was really good because all the things that had cropped up during the five days at home could go directly to her. One particular thing that came up was my phobia of birds, especially pheasants, which has become much worse, and we wondered whether it is related to other anxieties. She thinks it probably is, and suggested that it would be thought about more during the rest of my time here.

## Thursday 3 January

It's the start of 2008, so the theme in Creative Group was, 'What would you like to have in 2008 if you could rule the world?' I drew a black-and-white world with a shining glittery light coming from the corner. Because if anything this year, I want light to shine on my world, and show me the way forward to a new world in this New Year.

*The picture I drew in Creative Group – light shining on my world*

## Friday 4 January

I found out today that my second key worker isn't going to be there when I am discharged either – she is going to be on annual leave. So now, neither of my original key workers are going to be there. When I got in the car to go home with Mum and Dad I cried – key workers are meant to say goodbye to their key person, not the other way round.

## Saturday 5 January

In the morning we went school uniform shopping, but I was a bit anxious about it because I know that we are going because my old school uniform doesn't fit me any more. I was OK for most of it, but eventually it became too much and I realized that I needed to stop so I said–

'Can we go?'

–which Mum was fine about. I could feel myself going down a very negative track, and I had to get out before I started to compare myself or self-criticize my body even more. We got the uniform, though, which helped me feel more confident about going back to school, even if I wasn't feeling so confident on the inside.

What threw me slightly was having to eat my snacks in a café where we met my aunt, mostly because I wasn't expecting it. I got really worried about people looking at me and felt very self-conscious, especially because one of my snacks was chocolate and that is what I consider as a 'greedy food'. I just had to keep in mind how far I had come and how much courage I was showing by overcoming this challenge.

I have found it really hard to sleep at night recently. I spoke to Mum about it before I went to bed last night and we did some relaxation exercises to try to help me. I have also found that I've got a shortness of breath. It's happened in the past during quite stressful times for me – particularly in Year 6 when I was swimming with a club, doing gymnastics with another club, had exams, etc. So I guess it is not surprising that it has come back now when my key worker is leaving, I am starting school and I am being discharged – I guess it kind of all ties in.

Mum said that it helps her to relax if she thinks that she is outside a gate, and outside the gate is a tree you can leave all your worries and fears on. The world through the gate is a place where she loves to be, and she stays there until she is ready to leave. When she goes back through the gate her worries may still be there on the tree, or in a different place. It is then her choice whether to pick them up or to leave them there hanging on the tree.

I tried and tried to think of a truly happy place, a sanctuary, but I couldn't think of one where I had only happy memories. This makes me sad.

## Sunday 6 January

Today I relaxed and did some art. On the way back to hospital I was thinking about last night and how I couldn't think of a happy, safe place. I thought about my whole life, right from the very beginning to where I am now. I thought about my mum's womb, I know that sounds a bit (well, very) gross, but you're protected from the world, in a safe environment. I was loved even though my parents hadn't met me yet. I was no burden to anyone. You didn't have to worry about things because things couldn't worry you. Perhaps this was sanctuary . . .?

## Monday 7 January

I felt very fragile today. I'd put on what felt like loads of weight, and I was dreading this week in itself because my key worker is leaving and I had had hardly any sleep once again. I felt very low, but I just covered it up, I don't really know why. I think I just didn't want to open my box of worries because it was too painful, just too painful this week.

## Tuesday 8 January

There was a new admission today which was quite hard because it just pulls me back to the illness. On the other side, though, it reminds me that if I keep going the way I am, I will have a life, and I can achieve this goal. It is getting closer as every day passes.

> Dear Constance,
> hope this finds you well sweetheart. We were so sad to hear that you are going through some rough times but we know that down the road you will look back on these challenges and realise that they have made you a much stronger person.

*One of the letters that helped to keep me strong*

## Wednesday 9 January

In therapy we addressed my bird phobia. We discussed in particular how pheasants are wild birds and therefore quite unpredictable, which means that I am not in control, and can make me feel vulnerable. However, this fear is obviously affecting my life, and does feel uncontrollable. I am slowly losing one fear of food, but am increasing one of birds.

## Thursday 10 January

My key worker's leaving day. I couldn't believe that it was finally here. I had my last key session at noon. It was a chance to reflect on all of our memories, and value the special relationship that we have had.

When it was time for her to leave I just cried and cried. When we hugged goodbye I whispered, 'Please don't go.' She didn't reply.

I can't bear the thought that she has left. When someone has been so instrumental in helping you to rebuild your life, of course you don't want them to go. When I couldn't see a light, she held it there for me. She held hope for me when I was utterly hopeless and she kept me safe when I was scared and vulnerable. I will never forget what she has done for me, and how she has helped me to reshape and turn my life around.

## Friday 11 January

I felt really low today, grieving from the leaving of my key worker. Along with that there are now four people on the tube which brings back memories, painful memories. This brings the illness closer, which means I have to fight even harder to resist it. It also brings you down because you are having to fight so much of a mental battle inside. This makes me feel even more alone.

## Saturday 12 January

I had a school meeting today which was really helpful. My tutor[28] and I just went through what I would do in my free periods. This helped me to feel more relaxed about going back to school on Monday.

---

[28] My tutor at school helped my key teacher set the right amount of work for me, and would be there to support me when I came back to school.

## Sunday 13 January

Today I watched the two *Pride and Prejudice* films (to help with English) and then *Sense and Sensibility*, so it was a bit of a Jane Austen day!

## Monday 14 January

School today, my first day.[29] When I arrived there were loads of hugs, and it was great to see people, and sort of show them what their support has helped me do. At some points, though, the memories were excruciatingly painful, like walking past the loo where I use to go, or the bin where I use to hide food. It is a place in the past where I was blind to my destructive habits. I kept reassuring myself that this place that I am in now, after this voyage of discovery that I have been on, is where I want to be, and where I deserve to be. I found that this really helped me.

Lunch was hard because I felt really self-conscious about eating in front of people. I still don't want them to think that I am better. I just stayed focused, and it was definitely helpful deciding what I was going to have to eat in advance.

> TEXT MESSAGE:
> Constance. In all seriousness now I have never been so proud of someone. You have come so far and to see you back put an actual permanent smile on my face! I am so very proud of you.xxx

---

[29] When I started back at school, at first I stayed for the whole day, including lunch, but went back to the hospital after my lessons. Later, I stayed for after-school activities as well.

I spoke with my tutor at the end of the day to review how the day had gone. Overall I thought that it went well; it was challenging, but motivating, and I feel the 'p-word' . . . proud! Which I know now is a great feeling to have, and that everyone deserves to feel it, even me.

## Tuesday 15 January

A change was made at the hospital today. Anyone on the tube was going to have to sit on another table at lunchtime. I personally agree with this decision because coming back last night was like coming back to a house full of nothing but anorexia and unhelpful behaviours which right now, in my recovery, I really want to detach myself from as much as possible, because clinging on to it isn't going to help me.

## Wednesday 16 January

I announced my discharge today, which was so exciting. I feel proud, and when people congratulated me, I was able to own the compliments instead of pretending that they weren't for me, which feels really important, and something that I think I can value for the rest of my life of freedom.

---

TEXT MESSAGE:

Constance – Can I just say that I am never going to forget this day because this is the day that I can say without a shadow of doubt that you are the strongest and bravest person I know and ever will know. I will never forget the last year or so – it has taught me a lot. I am so proud of you sweetie. I still have every letter you sent me. I will keep them forever and one day show them to my kids and say this is what you can achieve when you try. Well done Constance! You better be proud. xxx

---

## Thursday 17 January

In Creative Group, I gained a real confidence boost because as a group we wrote down lots of things about each other, and the things that were said really touched me deep down, and kept me above my negative thoughts during quite a hard day for the community.

## Friday 18 January

I felt really unsupported today, but I am struggling to understand whether I'm actually not getting any support or whether I'm pushing it away, so that others who are struggling more than me can get the priority.

I guess that this question has come up in the past, although I haven't been able to name it directly. When I've been really struggling and felt hopeless, there was help and support all around, but my head refused to let me use it, although my heart could see it and wanted it. In contrast there have also been times when people were unable to help me, either because they couldn't understand or didn't know how to help me, or because it wasn't helpful support they were giving. I'm finding it hard that I can't distinguish between the two.

## Saturday 19 January

I found going to the gym really helpful today because it was such a good laugh, and it helped me to realize that exercising can be fun and an enjoyable experience, and that I don't have to think about it any more as a chore that I have to do.

## Sunday 20 January

I went to the cinema today with a friend from school. This was also great because I really cherish being normal. I feel like I am truly getting my life back on track, and that people like me not because I am anorexic, but because of other qualities that I hold. However, at present I am just not able to see them in myself. It feels too greedy to.

## Monday 21 January

I had an in-patient/out-patient handover meeting today which was good because it helped me to feel more reassured about the level of support that I will get when I leave.

However, I do feel extremely low because I didn't get a handover when I came back from school, only a talk with a new therapeutic care worker, who isn't even allowed to be allocated with anyone yet. This seems like a complete turnaround from Friday, when I felt like I was pushing support away, to now, when I want it but can't seem to get it. I feel like no one is really caring for me, and people are just letting me do my own thing. After all, I am leaving in three weeks, why would they still want to offer support to me? This question is going round and round in my mind, and all I can think of is that I am a bad person, which makes me feel even worse, and has sent me into a complete self-negative downward spiral, which I am in now – and because I don't feel anyone wants to listen to me, I am finding it hard to get out of it on my own. But who can I turn to?

## Tuesday 22 January

I did a key session today in which I wrote down all of the positives and negatives of leaving. I found this helpful – getting stuff down on paper helped me to clear my mind.

I'm feeling really mixed about the whole thing. Part of me is excited, and wants to move on and have a healthy, wonderful and exhilarating future; but on the other hand, the words 'moving on' seem like such big words. It's moving on into the unknown. In the future there is a chance that I will have a relapse, which I know I don't want – I don't want to come here again, but I am so scared that it will happen. What strangely links with that is that most of the dreams that I have been having recently are about anorexia – having a relapse, having to be transferred to another hospital, going back on the tube, getting really thin and dying, and all of these scare me, especially the last one, because it could have so easily come to that.

## Wednesday 23 January

In therapy we talked mostly about my discharge, and what I have gained from my time in hospital, and about my future.

The future is a scary thing because it's so unpredictable and so uncertain. The future is concealed from me, yet it knows that I am coming. I know that I can create my own future, but how much can anorexia also create?

## Thursday 24 January

After school today I did judo. This really helped me to get back into school life and interact with different people in a different environment. I felt accepted by my year group. They left my

122

difficulties and struggles behind, and consequently I was able to leave them behind too.

## Friday 25 January

I had two free periods today at school from where I dropped my two GCSEs. I found that I was able to take advantage of this, and start to catch up on my school work and feel comfortable with it. If people do judge me for it, that is OK, because I am learning to be my own individual, and to be grateful for what I do have. I haven't dropped the subjects because people don't think I am good enough to do them. I have missed a tremendous amount of time off school and therefore it is very valid for me to do this. This is such a shift for me, and such a nice space to be in.

After lessons I was also able to let myself relax and socialize with my friends. This was another change because I have never really done that before – I was always either exercising or working. I am starting to realize that people don't like me because I am a hard worker or enthusiastic about sport, they like me because I am me.

## Saturday 26 January

I helped out at a six-year-old's birthday party today and it really got me thinking about being a child. Living in a world where everything is magic. I admire young children's innocence and approach to things – they don't mind saying what they are feeling, and aren't scared of what their mind can do to them. Their innocence is their greatest virtue. But unfortunately we all have to grow up, and we enter a place where the magic is combated by logic and physics. Fairies don't actually live at the bottom of your garden, and adults aren't actually super-heroes! At least hope is there when you are young, and this stays with you for ever, no logic or physics can deny you this, and it is only when you are older that you can actually use it to its greatest advantage.

## Sunday 27 January

I didn't do much today, but instead I was up all night worrying about school tomorrow. I am still really insecure about myself. What if people don't like me . . . ? What if they are just being nice to my face . . . ? And still the question remains about whether people are judging me for dropping some of my GCSEs. I tried to calm myself down and relax myself by thinking of all the beautiful texts, letters and words of support that people have given me. That helped me to realize that the support is genuine and it is because people cared for me when I couldn't care for myself.

## Monday 28 January

School was OK, a bit tough, but that is to be expected. Although this time I faced one of my biggest challenges so far . . . I went swimming. It was such a huge thing. I saw it as an option after school and something just came over me . . . I was going to do it, I can't keep putting it off for ever. I used to do it four times a week. It was made easier because there weren't any boys, and also no one from my year was there, so I felt like the other years might not judge me as much, if they did judge me on my size. It was hard putting my costume on and looking down and being so appalled by my body.

*'Look what they did . . . they made you fat.'*

'NO! They made me healthy. I was malnourished before.' I told myself that I wasn't even going to have this conversation with myself and it stopped there.

Once I was in the water, though, I was OK because I felt concealed. The sense of achievement I felt afterwards was so huge. I don't think that I showed it much on the outside, but inside I was jumping for delight, and I still am. I so prefer the space that I am in, it is so much better than where I was before. To feel this happy is worth every bit of pain and hurt that I endured to get here.

I felt that Mum was quite forceful afterwards, though, with getting me to eat extra. I felt like she was taking away from me what I had just achieved. I didn't like it, I felt like I was being pushed into a corner, which meant I felt like I had to refuse food, so we argued about that. I felt really uncomfortable, but we were able to talk to each other directly, which helped us understand each other. Mum was concerned about me exercising again, and getting into an obsessive habit again, and I can understand that – she is scared. For me various things had happened at school which made the illness greater for me and made me realize that it is still a big part of me. For example, someone said,

'Ah, I'm starving, I haven't had any breakfast.'

All I heard was 'no breakfast' and I wished that it could have been me, but I had to stop and think about where that would get me. Another thing was when people were handing around food at break. I wanted to take it so I could fit in more, but I can't let myself because if I do then I'm acknowledging that I am 'better'.

These two things in particular had made me feel insecure; and so on top of that, being pressured meant that I had to refuse food. Mum and I talked and worked through my anxieties, and she was able to understand what I was finding hard. Talking really helped in this situation.

## Tuesday 29 January

When I came back to the hospital today I had a handover with a member of staff who I don't really know and don't trust, so I didn't really talk about the true ups and downs of the weekend. This got me thinking about my out-patient team because I don't know them very well and so I don't trust them, and in order to make sure that I don't relapse their support is going to be vital, but I don't know how to break this lack of trust.

## Wednesday 30 January

In therapy we talked about my time at home and the events that occurred. Especially the 'no breakfast' remark at school. The therapist explained that I wasn't able to take into consideration that whoever said that will probably have extra food at lunch to make up for their hunger; I was only able to see the 'no eating' part of it.

My therapist also said how proud she was of me for going swimming. It felt uplifting to get that positive response from someone, because I remember a time when I couldn't allow myself to feel pride, and I didn't even let other people hold it for me.

## Thursday 31 January

In Creative Group, we continued to work on our pieces about each other. Mine was read out. It was so lovely to hear such kind and encouraging things said about me, and it really does make you feel special, and cherished by other people.

Most likely to become!
A Teacher
Something to do with maths
A Judge, (in court)
Accountant or Surfer!

3 Words to Sum them Up!
Knowledgeable, Organised
Intelligent, Talented, Caring, Clever,
Surfboard, Brave, Sweet, Funny,
Surfing, thoughtful, Trusting,
Groovy!

One Thing I admire!
Her ability to speak her
mind and how she feels
Speaking your mind,
Determination and
genuineness

How you make me Smile!
Sense of humour, being a
juke box! Hilarious
Comments!
Your giggle! Your slight
gullibility!

What they're good at!
Knowing how to cheer me up 😊
And always a caring ear to listen!
Maths and giving advice
Playing the piano, chatting and
making you feel welcome, relaxed
and calming people down.

Fave Memory!
Making me laugh at Halloween!
Sharing a room and late
night chats
Run away from the bee in the
bathroom!
'Shake it Off'-heehee!

Something We Share!
Wanting to do well at school.
Thoughts and feelings around
the illness. Liking water sports
Telling people what we
really think.
Laughing at ourselves!

*The sheet that was made for me by the other young people in Creative Group*

## Friday 1 February

Lunch at school was really hard because of the anticipation that grew inside me and the anxieties became overwhelming. I just had to keep thinking of my achievements so far, and where I still want to get to, and know that I am stronger and that is what helped me through, but all the way through my illness was so strong:

*'Don't eat, let me back in your life, you were thin, comfortable and beautiful with me and I valued your dedication to me.'*

It was so powerful at lunch, but actually people's dedication to me felt so much better, and that was much more powerful and got me through.

## Saturday 2 February

My lessons finished at 11 a.m. and I made the decision to go home, which was quite a big step. I didn't feel the need to stay and work, and I was able to have the rest of the day to myself and enjoy doing the things that I want to do, rather than should do, because I have never allowed myself to do that before.

## Sunday 3 February

I went to buy some materials for my Leaving Group[30] and it really hit me that I was leaving hospital after seven months. I feel that I am ready to leave, but it is the friendships that I am going to leave behind that I am really going to miss, and the support network.

---

[30] When you are discharged you have a Leaving Group with all the other young people where you can decide what you want to do – some people play games, for example, while others do creative activities. I wanted to do something creative, so I bought a canvas and some paints.

## Monday 4 February

Swimming was harder today because there were boys. It made me feel more self-conscious, especially when I had to get out of the pool in front of them. Part of me knows that I don't need to be so self-conscious because I am not fat, but it is such a tiny part that it didn't shine through enough to combat my negative thoughts.

## Tuesday 5 February

I was meant to see my other original key worker for a key session today, but she was ill which means that I am never going to see her again, now she's going on leave. This really saddens me because she has helped me so much and I wanted to say goodbye. I might be able to have a phone call some time though.

## Wednesday 6 February

I met with a member of staff today to fill out some psychology forms, so they can compare them with when I first came in. They were mostly related to food and feelings around eating. It was good for me to see where I was still struggling, like rules in my head such as finding it hard to eat extra. Although it was good to see where I have come from, it also seems very daunting because it feels like everything is hard in one way or another. I know that I am not going to be completely better when I leave, and I have known that for a long time, but it's hard not to be put down by that. For example, one of the questions was,

'When you exercise do you think about calories or weight loss?'

I couldn't say no, because I do think about it, but I don't exercise now because of it, I do it for my enjoyment now. But because I couldn't say no, I felt like I was completely obsessed. I guess it links with my black-and-white thinking, like you are good or bad, fat or thin. Everything needs to be perfect, which I can see isn't healthy, but I don't know how to control it.

## Thursday 7 February

I had my last family therapy session today. We talked about things that can 'feed my anorexia' and how I want to be treated normally and get rid of my anorexic tag, but also want people to realize that I am still ill. I can't forget that power that you get, and what an invigorating feeling it is when you don't eat and are in control. It's like my safety net in the back of my head, but I know if I use it a hole will form and I'll just drop straight through it into nowhere. I have to trust myself.

## Friday 8 February

I was the last finishing lunch at school today which made me feel good. I didn't feel greedy. I know that this is an unhealthy thought process, but it just comes naturally. What scares me, though, is that I still find it really hard to eat in front of my school friends, and I am leaving hospital in a week. How can I break this barrier?

## Saturday 9 February

An issue came up at lunch. We were meant to be having pizza, but Mum was worried about the calories, and whether she should work it out exactly. I said that this was probably the worst thing that she could do because I'm constantly counting calories, so working them out and worrying about them is an example of 'feeding my anorexia'. I just took a healthy-looking portion, and managed that without needing to know the exact amount of calories.

## Sunday 10 February

It struck me today, while I was writing my leaving cards, that I have only got four days left. I'm very mixed about leaving with so many different emotions – fear, excitement, worry, confusion, relief. What I did realize especially today was how much courage all us young people are showing, and what bravery it takes to face your difficulties, and I am probably never going to meet such strong-minded people in my life.

## Monday 11 February

When I was at school last week I asked my tutor whether I could see my challenge grades.[31] She said no because it was not appropriate, and I can understand why, but I felt a bit over-protected by this. I talked about it with my key teacher, and I feel in a bit of a dilemma about it. On the one hand, the grades are there to motivate students, and I certainly don't need motivation. Also, I can see myself getting back into a 'work, work, work' habit because nothing will be good enough. On the other hand, I can't be protected for ever, and I have to see them one day.

## Tuesday 12 February

On my phone call I got into a bit of a disagreement with my dad because he and Mum had made the decision to give gifts to some of my core team but not others. I didn't feel that this was right because they were leaving out my therapist, who has probably

---

[31] This is the system my school uses, in which you are given a grade to work for. This is called the 'challenge grade'.

done the most work with me, and helped me challenge my thoughts the most, along with my key workers. I feel cross that they didn't include me in their decision; after all, I am the one who has worked directly with them. What made it worse was that my dad just raised his voice and started speaking faster, because he thinks that means I will take his point of view – and it doesn't, it means I retreat, so then I am not able to say directly to him what I am feeling, so that doesn't help any of us. I wish he would put some of the work that we have done into practice.

> 12 Feb.
>
> Dear Constance – just a note to wish you strength and courage in the next phase of your life. I imagine your self-learning has been enormous over the past few months, I hope you can continue to build on it all and find the right way ahead for you in the future.
>
> All the very best of everything for you. Much love ████ X.

*A letter from my godmother just before my discharge*

## Wednesday 13 February

My penultimate day. I met with the same member of staff to go through the forms. It was really encouraging to see the progress that I had made from when I came.

In the evening all of the young people watched *Sister Act 1* and *2*. I enjoyed spending time with everyone, because I am never going to do it again. I am going to miss the friendships that I have made, and I am going to treasure the support that these amazingly special, talented young people have given me.

## Thursday 14 February

Oh my goodness . . . this is it. Today I left the hospital.

I awoke full of excitement, but the reality of it slowly sank in during the day.

Morning Meeting was really emotional, all these things that I have now done for the last time. The warmth that the community seemed to give me could cure any illness. For the first time I really felt that people cared for me. They valued my presence, and liked me and accepted me for who I am. I feel protected here, and part of me doesn't want to leave this nest of security.

I got to choose my last leaving lunch. I chose cottage pie and broccoli because it was my first ever meal here, all the way back in July. It's like a circle. My leaving theme is Rings, because they symbolize many things for me. For one thing, I always wear two rings. One is the one that the young person gave me to say good luck when my tube came out. The other one is the one that my parents got me when we went out one weekend. They are quite important for me because I have a habit of spinning them when something is worrying me, so I guess they have also helped the

14th Feb 0F

My dearest Constance
When I think of the
battles you have faced
& of your determination
to overcome your fears
& doubts, I am filled
with awe & wonder, that
someone, so young, can
have conquered so
much.

Constance, you are

*The letter my mum and dad wrote to me the day I left hospital*

an amazing young
woman. We can all
see it. And perhaps now
you'll begin to believe it
too, That people are
surrounding you with so
much love and support
because you are you.

Keep going, you have much
to hold up your head
high, be proud of yourself

    With all love & blessings,
    Mum & Dad xxx

Start saving for Hawaii!

staff a bit! Rings symbolize support circles and being surrounded by love. God is also circling me.

My case manager and I both gave our speeches. She went first:

'When you told me what your theme was for today I was thinking about the meaning of rings and circles and wanted to include this in my speech, so here it goes!

'When you first came to hospital nearly seven months ago now, I remember you as being very quiet and it seemed that you were often on the edge or separate from the circles at the hospital, preferring to be on your own. It seemed that anorexia had played a part, as it does with many young people, in keeping you separated from some really important circles – circles of people and learning, and at home with your family – and it wanted to do the same when you arrived at the hospital.

'Over time and through a process of trusting and being invited and reassured, you were able to begin to join some smaller circles, moving on to the larger group, and to be involved in the really important journey of learning about yourself through others. This has involved being part of circular processes such as being a good friend and allowing others to be a good friend to you, giving and receiving feedback and support and learning that you can express unhappiness or annoyance with others and they can respond in a way other than you fear. Joining these circles has allowed you to begin to see and us to share the really special qualities that make you who you are and for you to shine as an individual. I wanted to concentrate on the elements that make you Constance despite your achievements (although these are also important) as these can often be the hardest bits to hold on to.

'Just a few examples of these are:

'Being really thoughtful and caring and reaching out to others.

'Expressing and holding on to your own views even when they are different from others (a really good sign of being confident in yourself).

'Always giving things a go! When things don't look interesting at first glance or you have a scary task to tackle, you are always ready to get stuck in and make the best of things – a quality that will stand you in good stead for the future. Also being able to make people laugh both unintentionally and intentionally, a memorable example being when you shared with the group in school how you felt "gutted . . . like a fish in Tesco's!!!!!"

'These and many other qualities will go with you on the next part of your journey as you rejoin and become part of new circles, continuing to learn about and gain confidence in yourself both including and despite of your achievements.

'So finally, on behalf of everyone at the hospital I want to wish you lots of strength and happiness and wish you and your family all the best for the future.'

Then it was my turn:

'I remember travelling in the car almost exactly seven months ago to be admitted to hospital. I didn't really know where I was going. I didn't really know much about my illness, but most of all I didn't really know much about myself and who I really was.

'My time here for me feels a bit like I have been on my surfboard in a rough storm, and only recently have the waves started to subside, but now that the worst of the storm is over, I feel so much stronger to continue fighting outside of here, because while I've been here, I've realigned my priorities, and being ill certainly isn't one of them any more.

'The support here is incredible, especially from the amazing staff – you really do help to turn young people's lives around, and I really do appreciate every bit of it, and to the young people, just keep going because we *all* deserve so much better than illness and I'm going to miss everyone here so much.'

In my Leaving Group I had a gold canvas and I got people to do hand prints on it. I wanted them to do this so that I had something to take away with me, and it reflects on all our individualities.

When it is time to leave everyone makes a tunnel going from the door, so you hug everyone and then go under everyone's arms out of the door. Everyone in that tunnel had contributed to my recovery.

So that was it – it was goodbye to hospital and anorexia and I welcome my future with a sense of positivity and self-belief. I am now closer to my future than I was yesterday, and I know that I can do this . . .

# AFTER DISCHARGE
## August 2009

That was my journey through hospital as an in-patient in an eating disorders unit. You have read my hopelessness and hopefulness. You have read each of my diligent steps through recovery from anorexia.

I have done amazingly well since being discharged and the devil of anorexia has no power over me. Yes, very, very, occasionally some days are still hard, and I do want to return to it, but I can't. I don't want to be remembered now as the anorexic, or the girl with the tube; instead I want to be known as Constance. I love being free, and I am now living the life that I have always imagined.

When I think back, I often can't believe that I have got to this point. Two years ago all I wanted to do was starve myself to death, in the belief that it would make me a better person. When I read that article in the newspaper in September, I thought that anorexia would be something that I would just have to put up with and base my life around, but in actual fact, now it isn't part of my life at all – apart from in a positive way, by raising awareness. I am now a

Young Ambassador for Beat[1] which means that, by working with the media, I try to help change the stereotypes that people face when suffering from an eating disorder. I love not having to live by inner rules and I love understanding myself and feeling comfortable with who I am. Ironically, instead of seeking happiness by trying to fulfil my previous desires, I have found my happiness by restricting them.

After my discharge I met with my out-patient therapist once a week. The first time I saw her was a few days after I'd left hospital and I didn't really want to see her, so the session was very awkward. I didn't want to have to make new connections; it just felt like another thing to have to do. But you can't tell people about how you are feeling until you trust them, so first I had to learn to trust her. It helped to think that I would much rather be meeting someone from an out-patient team than being an in-patient again. Once we had built up a relationship the support was invaluable, and it has been one of the reasons why I've been able to stay healthy.

The work of the out-patient staff was to maintain me through recovery, but I began this long journey in hospital. The staff there were so fantastic, and although we gave them little gifts when I left, no presents will never repay them for what they have done and supported me through – their work is priceless. They fought with me against anorexia. And they helped me to win.

When I was discharged I didn't follow a meal plan, nor was I

---

[1] Beat is the working name of the Eating Disorders Association, which works to raise awareness and understanding about eating disorders and to help people overcome them.

weighed. We talked this through with my out-patient team and my parents and we all felt that it was the right decision for me. I had worked really hard at trying to detach myself from weights and figures, and I knew from the moment I walked out of the doors of the hospital that I wanted to lead a normal life. I understood that if there were any doubts about my health then I would need to be weighed and go back on to a meal plan. Inside me, though, I had enough self-belief to know that it wouldn't be necessary. However, I've had to realize that some parts of my life I won't be able to return to. I am now doing exercise in a normal healthy way, yet running is just too dangerous a trigger for me. I started running in competitions again and qualifying for further races, but it started to unbalance me, and it was just too much of a risk, so I had to pull out. Although this makes me sad and I really want to be able to continue to run, I just have to accept that it is too dangerous for me to return to it.

My life since discharge hasn't always been an easy ride, and it is important to note that I did suffer a relapse for about two months around Christmas time 2008. The voice crept back in and I started excessively exercising again in secret. My mum instinctively knew that something was wrong and was vigilant and tried to find a way for me to open up, but I just kept pushing her away and saying that I was fine. It took about two weeks for me to acknowledge that I was slipping back down into my destructive habits, but because of the work I had done in hospital I was able to recognize what was happening, and I finally took the decision to confide in my mum. Immediately my support network stepped up again and I was able to come through it.

I would imagine that it is common for a relapse to occur during recovery, and it is essential to remember that if you suffer a relapse it doesn't mean that you are a bad person, or that you have let people around you down, because you haven't. I remember feeling such a huge guilt because of all the effort that people had put into helping me, but actually recovery is such a huge task, and *no one* is expecting it to be plain sailing. Also, if you do experience a relapse, it doesn't mean that things will go back to the way they were, because I think somewhere inside you realize that you don't want to go back to anorexia, and in fact it was my memories of how bad things were that helped to get me through. Unlike the first time when my mum took me to the doctor, when I was so cross with her because I didn't want any help, this time was different, and I was very grateful for the extra support, and that my appointments with my out-patient therapist could easily be increased depending on how I was feeling. It was also really helpful when both my therapist and my parents said to me, 'We will *not* let you get ill again.' In fact, we didn't name it as a relapse; we just referred to it as a small dip in my recovery – which, to be honest, is how I would also describe it. Acknowledging what was happening was the first step, and because I was able to do this, the healthy side of me was able to get stronger and stronger again, and within a couple of months the anorexia had left me – for the last time.

I've learnt to balance my time between work and social time. More importantly, I have realized that I am not defined by my exam grades, and that people don't like me or dislike me because of my academic work. I went back to school normally, and it was really helpful that my school didn't put any pressure on me to perform academically, and not having my challenge grades helped

144

me not to make school work an obsession again. The same arrangement applied for sport: if I was having a hard day it wasn't compulsory for me to attend sport. I saw my tutor individually every week, and we reviewed the week and how I was managing school life. All of this support at school was really beneficial and helped me feel secure during the days. I managed to catch up on all of the work that I missed, and now I am so relieved that I didn't take ten GCSEs because it wouldn't have been possible – it would have been totally unrealistic to attempt it while I was trying to stay focused on recovery after discharge. It didn't make sense at the time, but I now understand that my health is far more important than exam grades and numbers. In the end I did really well in my GCSEs and I was very happy. However, if they hadn't come out as I wanted, then although I think I would have been disappointed for a couple of days, and possibly sad for longer, I'm pretty sure that I would have been able to get over it, because I now don't judge myself on academic results – and I've got my health back.

I know that I have got amazing friends and family. They were, and still are, so supportive. My parents were so unswerving in their love for me, and they always believed that I would get better – not that I could get better; that I *would* get better. So although sometimes I got annoyed with them, the fact that they believed in me was what counted. We grew and blossomed as a family and learnt to be open with each other about how we were feeling. However, shockingly, just over a year after my discharge, in March 2009 my dad was diagnosed with terminal cancer, and he died less than three months later. Yet even out of this tragedy and my everlasting grief I hope that I am able to take one positive thing – I hope that this shows that it is possible to stay healthy and strong throughout the most extreme and hardest of adversities. This harrowing experience has shown me that I don't need anorexia as a safety net any more. When the horrible news about his illness came, I didn't immediately return to my eating disorder for security – in fact, it was the last thing on my mind, because I knew that I wanted to spend as much time as possible with my dad, and I certainly didn't want to spend it wrapped in anorexia. This has now proved to me that I am fully recovered from my eating disorder. My dad was such an important part of my recovery and he helped me in so many ways to get through my illness; I just wish that there was some way in which I could have helped save him from his illness. In a sad and twisted way, at least I can now say that we are both free of our suffering from our illnesses, and I know that he is always with me.

For anyone suffering from anorexia, I want you to know that there is always hope. Even when you feel like you are trapped inside the prison of anorexia, there is always a key to unlock the door and let yourself out. It will take time, and patience, and the urge to get better won't come overnight. But honestly, it will come one day. Let others hold hope there for you if you don't feel able to see it.

Putting weight on is possibly the hardest part about recovery, but, just as I had to learn that I am not defined by my academic work, I also had to learn that I am not judged by my weight. Your weight is just a number, and that number isn't who you are. It is just a number. I used to hate it when people said to me, 'You look really good,' or 'You look a lot better,' because I just interpreted that as *'I look fat.'* It helped me to think really hard about what I actually saw and what other people saw, and to realize that people

146

were only trying to be nice when they said those things, and it was my anorexia which was interpreting those comments in a different way. Along with that, I started to feel so much better physically. I didn't faint, my muscles didn't ache, I wasn't tired and I was able to do more things. The things I love. Finally, the professionals won't, and will never, let you get 'fat' – they will make you healthy again. It is such a negative and harmful word that can unbalance people so easily, and yet actually it isn't important at all because you should feel proud and confident with who you are. If you try to keep all these positive things in mind it really does help. Use the support of others around you, because they are there to help you. You have the strength inside you to carry on. I want you to get to where I am now – and I know that you can. Believe in yourself. You can.

My true identity has finally revealed itself to me. I am now the author and decision-maker of my life; anorexia is not, and it never will be again.

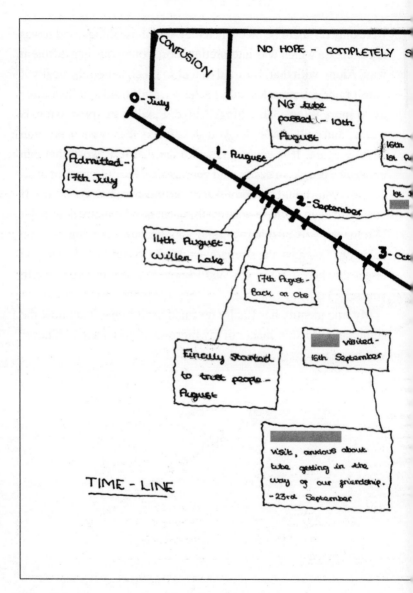

*Timeline: key stages on my road to recovery*

148

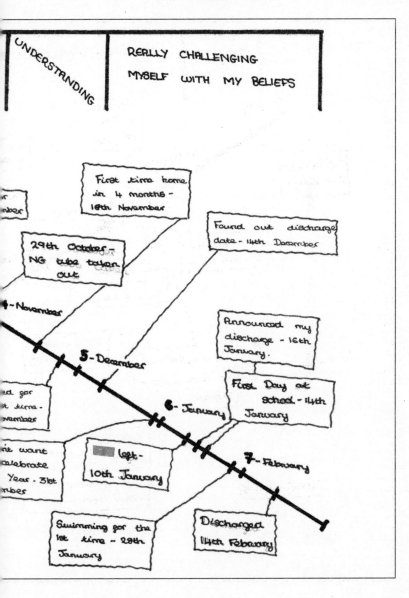

UNDERSTANDING

REALLY CHALLENGING
MYSELF WITH MY BELIEFS

First time home
in 4 months -
16th November

29th October -
NG tube taken
out

...ber

4 - November

Found out discharge
date - 14th December

Announced my
discharge - 16th
January.

5 - December

First Day at
school - 14th
January

6 - January

...d for
...t time -
...vember

... left -
10th January

7 - February

...t want
...alebrate
...Year - 31st
...ber

Swimming for the
1st time - 28th
January

Discharged
14th February

# APPENDIX: USEFUL CONTACTS AND FURTHER READING

## Useful Contacts
Beat (the Eating Disorders Association):
www.b-eat.co.uk/Home
Helpline: 08456 341414; help@b-eat.co.uk
Youthline (for under-18s): 08456 347650;
fyp@b-eat.co.uk; TXT: 07786 201820

ChildLine (24 hours – free and confidential): 0800 1111;
www.childline.org.uk.
Confidential one-to-one online chat with a ChildLine counsellor
and private email are available via the website.

## Further Reading
*Anorexia: A Stranger in the Family* by Katie Metcalfe (Accent
Press, 2006)

*Anorexia and Bulimia in the Family: One Parent's Practical Guide to Recovery* by Gráinne Smith (Wiley Blackwell, 2003)

*Anorexia Nervosa: A Survival Guide for Families, Friends and Sufferers* by Janet Treasure (Psychology Press, 1997)

*Eating Disorders: A Parents' Guide* by Rachel Bryant-Waugh and Bryan Lask (Routledge, 2004)

*Overcoming Anorexia Nervosa* by Christopher Freeman (Robinson, 2009)

*Overcoming Bulimia Nervosa and Binge-Eating* by Peter Cooper (Robinson, 2009)

# The Compassionate Mind
*A New Approach to Life's Challenges*

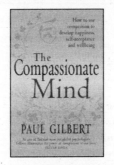

**Develop your feelings of compassion and increase your sense of well-being.**

In societies that encourage us to compete with each other, compassion is often seen as a weakness. Striving to get ahead, self-criticism, fear and hostility towards others seem to come more naturally to us. *The Compassionate Mind* reveals the evolutionary and social reasons why our brains react so readily to threats and how research has shown that our brains are also hardwired to respond to kindness and compassion.

Research has found that developing kindness and compassion for ourselves and others builds our confidence, helps us create meaningful, caring relationships and promotes physical and mental health. Far from fostering emotional weakness, practical exercises focusing on developing compassion have been found to subdue our anger and increase our courage and resilience to depression and anxiety.

'This wise and perceptive book teaches us self-compassion and the consolations of kindness. I recommend it all the time.'
    — Sally Brampton, author of *Shoot the Damn Dog: A Memoir of Depression* and the Aunt Sally column in the *Sunday Times*

**Professor Paul Gilbert** is the author of *Overcoming Depression*, which has sold more than 135,000 copies, and is Professor of Clinical Psychology at the University of Derby and Director of the Mental Health Research Unit, Kingsway Hospital, Derby.

978-1-84901-098-6
£9.99

Visit www.constablerobinson.com for more information

## More psychology titles from Constable & Robinson
### Please visit www.overcoming.co.uk for more information

| No. | Title | RRP | Offer price | Total |
|-----|-------|-----|-------------|-------|
| | An Introduction to Coping with Anxiety | £2.99 | £2.00 | |
| | An Introduction to Coping with Depression | £2.99 | £2.00 | |
| | An Introduction to Coping with Health Anxiety | £2.99 | £2.00 | |
| | An Introduction to Coping with Obsessive Compulsive Disorder | £2.99 | £2.00 | |
| | An Introduction to Coping with Panic | £2.99 | £2.00 | |
| | An Introduction to Coping with Phobias | £2.99 | £2.00 | |
| | Overcoming Anger and Irritability | £10.99 | £8.99 | |
| | Overcoming Anorexia Nervosa | £10.99 | £8.99 | |
| | Overcoming Anxiety | £10.99 | £8.99 | |
| | Overcoming Anxiety Self-Help Course (3 parts) | £21.00 | £18.00 | |
| | Overcoming Body Image Problems | £10.99 | £8.99 | |
| | Overcoming Bulimia Nervosa and Binge-Eating – new edition | £10.99 | £8.99 | |
| | Overcoming Bulimia Nervosa and Binge-Eating Self-Help Course (3 parts) | £21.00 | £18.00 | |
| | Overcoming Childhood Trauma | £10.99 | £8.99 | |
| | Overcoming Chronic Fatigue | £10.99 | £8.99 | |
| | Overcoming Chronic Pain | £10.99 | £8.99 | |
| | Overcoming Compulsive Gambling | £10.99 | £8.99 | |
| | Overcoming Depersonalizaton and Feelings of Unreality | £10.99 | £8.99 | |
| | Overcoming Depression – new edition | £10.99 | £8.99 | |
| | Overcoming Depression: Talks With Your Therapist (audio) | £10.99 | £8.99 | |
| | Overcoming Grief | £10.99 | £8.99 | |
| | Overcoming Health Anxiety | £10.99 | £8.99 | |
| | Overcoming Insomnia and Sleep Problems | £10.99 | £8.99 | |
| | Overcoming Low Self-Esteem | £10.99 | £8.99 | |
| | Overcoming Low Self-Esteem Self-Help Course (3 parts) | £21.00 | £18.00 | |
| | Overcoming Mood Swings | £10.99 | £8.99 | |
| | Overcoming Obsessive Compulsive Disorder | £10.99 | £8.99 | |
| | Overcoming Panic and Agoraphobia | £10.99 | £8.99 | |
| | Overcoming Panic and Agoraphobia Self-Help Course (3 parts) | £21.00 | £18.00 | |
| | Overcoming Paranoid and Suspicious Thoughts | £10.99 | £8.99 | |

# More psychology titles from Constable & Robinson

| No. | Title | RRP | Offer price | Total |
|---|---|---|---|---|
| | Overcoming Problem Drinking | £10.99 | £8.99 | |
| | Overcoming Relationship Problems | £10.99 | £8.99 | |
| | Overcoming Sexual Problems | £10.99 | £8.99 | |
| | Overcoming Social Anxiety and Shyness | £10.99 | £8.99 | |
| | Overcoming Social Anxiety and Shyness Self-Help Course (3 parts) | £21.00 | £18.00 | |
| | Overcoming Stress | £10.99 | £8.99 | |
| | Overcoming Traumatic Stress | £10.99 | £8.99 | |
| | Overcoming Weight Problems | £10.99 | £8.99 | |
| | Overcoming Worry | £10.99 | £8.99 | |
| | Overcoming Your Child's Fears and Worries | £10.99 | £8.99 | |
| | Overcoming Your Child's Shyness and Social Anxiety | £10.99 | £8.99 | |
| | Overcoming Your Smoking Habit | £10.99 | £8.99 | |
| | The Compassionate Mind | £9.99 | £7.99 | |
| | The Happiness Trap | £9.99 | £7.99 | |
| | The Glass Half-Full | £8.99 | £7.99 | |
| | I Had a Black Dog | £6.99 | £5.24 | |
| | Living with a Black Dog | £7.99 | £5.99 | |
| | Manage Your Mood: How to use Behavioral Activation Techniques to Overcome Depression | £12.99 | £9.99 | |
| | P&P | | FREE | FREE |
| | TOTAL | | | |

Name (block letters): _____

Address: _____

_____ Postcode: _____

Email: _____ Tel No: _____

How to Pay:
1. By telephone: call the TBS order line on 01206 255 800 and quote SCOTT. Phone lines are open between Monday–Friday, 8.30am–5.30pm.

2. By post: send a cheque for the full amount payable to TBS Ltd, and send form to: Freepost RLUL-SJGC-SGKJ. Cash Sales/Direct Mail Dept, The Book Service, Colchester Road, Frating, Colchester, CO7 7DW

Is/are the book(s) intended for personal use ☐ or professional use ☐ ?
Please note this information will not be passed on to third parties.